Move Our Message

D1456192

OCT 2012

Move Our Message

How to Get America's Ear

Susan C. Strong

THE METAPHOR PROJECT

The Metaphor Project, P.O. Box 892, Orinda, CA 94563
TEL 925-254-7198, FAX 925-254-3304
metaphorproject@earthlink.net

Editor: Dalya F. Massachi, Writing for Community Success
Book design: Sharon Constant, Visible Ink Design
Cover Design: Susan Strong and Sharon Constant
Author photo: Robert Mackinlay Photography
Printed and bound in the United States of America

ISBN 9780615548777
Library of Congress Control Number 2011917461

Publisher's Cataloging-in-Publication
(Provided by Quality Books, Inc.)

Strong, Susan C.
    Move our message : how to get America's ear / by
Susan C. Strong. — 1st ed.
      p. cm.
    Includes bibliographical references.
    LCCN 2011917461
    ISBN-13: 9780615548777
    ISBN-10: 0615548776

    1. Communication in politics—United States.
    2. Communication in marketing—United States.
    3. Progressivism (United States politics)   I. Title.

JA85.2.U6S77 2012   320.973'01'4
                          QBI11-600201

To RDS, always my first reader

CONTENTS

"The organizer, in his constant hunt for patterns, universalities, and meaning, is always building up a body of experience...It is essential for communication that he know of [his audience's] experiences....He learns the local legends, anecdotes, values, idioms. He listens to small talk. He refrains from rhetoric foreign to the local culture..."

— Saul Alinsky, *Rules for Radicals*

"I think there is a hesitancy to talk using populist language," the Ohio Democrat said in a sit-down interview with *The Huffington Post*. "I think it has to do with a sort of intellectual elitism that considers that kind of talk is somehow lacking in sophistication. I'm not sure where it comes from. But I think it's there. There's an unwillingness to draw a line in the sand."

— Ted Strickland, narrowly defeated Ohio Governor on
Democratic losses in the 2010 election, quoted in
"Democrats Suffering from 'Intellectual Elitism,'"
by Sam Stein, *The Huffington Post*, *12.01.10*

"Are we conveying a coherent vision of the world (a framework) to the public, are we drawing on lessons and metaphors they know and understand, are we explaining how a progressive position connects to basic American values?"

— Susan Nall Bales, in an online essay entitled
"Reframing Community Messages through Myths
and Metaphors," (found at: *www.c3.ucla.edu/tool-
box/terms-concepts/strategic-frame-analysis/
reframing-community-messages-through-myths-and-metaphors).*

"[My] book is a vision of a movement for the conscious evolution of increasingly conscious social systems — a movement of activists dedicated to calling forth new social systems. These are new forms of economics, politics, governance, and cultural stories that are increasingly aligned with the realities of nature and humanity. These conscious evolutionary activists realize that such social systems would not constitute an ideal utopian state, but would rather be endlessly imperfect, like the universe, yet capable of their own ongoing evolution..."

— Tom Atlee, *Reflections on Evolutionary Activism*

Introduction

Today our economy, our environment, and our health face more threats than ever. We desperately need smart new ways to address those threats. Although local grassroots, bottom-up approaches are vital now, we also must create an effective national effort. The 2008 election had given us hope that progressive ideas for change would get heard in Washington, D.C. Now we know it will take a very hard fight to make that happen. Even more than a sometimes-friendly president, we need a willing Congress. Getting Congress on our side depends on citizen pressure heavy enough to outweigh big corporate dollars and Tea Party types.

FDR once said to the renowned labor organizer, A. Phillip Randolph: "...I agree with everything you've said [about what you want]...but I would ask one thing of you, Mr. Randolph, and that is, go out and make me do it."[1] Today, making our politicians do what we (and sometimes they themselves) might like requires a lot more visible public demand than FDR needed. Success at creating that kind of pressure depends on savvy, mainstream-accessible American Framing.

American Framing is a way of translating our own ideals, values, stories, and policy goals into colorful political language that spreads.[2] Most Americans understand phrases like "let's move forward," "play by the rules," or "can do." Everyday metaphors and short phrases like these form part of our enduring political lexicon. They evoke our ideal national identity as a people. Using quintessential American political words like "change" and "yes, we can" helped give the Democrats victory in 2008. Many feel that the lack of this kind of framing contributed to Democratic defeat in 2010.

Regardless of whether those 2008 sound bites actually brought us the change they promised, their political success in that election validates again the findings of modern cognitive science: storytelling language works best here.[3] More specifically, American storytelling language works best. This remains true whether or not election year promises have been kept. Over the long history of our republic, some may have used American Framing to promise more than they could deliver, or to mislead and even to outright lie. But we must use it to tell the truth. This book will show you how to do American Framing with integrity and success.

Even if you already use The Metaphor Project's online resources at *www.metaphorproject.org*, what follows will provide you with new help in framing your messages for mainstream Americans. The chapters ahead offer the most up-to-date, in-depth, and sequential presentation of what American Framing is, why it works, and how to do it. The first four chapters will be especially useful for persuading your progressive colleagues and friends to try it too.

In Part I, you'll find out more about the rationale for American Framing and explore one of our key resources for evoking The Ideal American Identity Story. Also included in Part I are a section on how to answer common objections to "speaking American," and a chapter describing the intuitive process some American activists followed in creating powerful new political metaphors. This chapter lays vital groundwork for Parts II and III, because it demonstrates the kind of mental process that underlies The Metaphor Project's American Framing Steps.

Part II: More American Frames That Stuck includes key Metaphor Project examples with short case histories and the web essays that made them go viral. At critical moments in the last decade, these widely forwarded pieces made important American story suggestions for a range of peace, justice, and environmental issues. But that's not all.

In Part III: How to Frame It American, I provide a detailed introduction and walk-through of The Metaphor Project's American

Framing Steps. This newly revised material substantially updates and enriches the resources featured on our website over the years. Part III is the business end of the book—the place where the rubber meets the road—all presented in a handy format that doesn't require booting up or printing out. (It won't suddenly disappear, either, should anything happen to the Internet!) In this section I explain the hidden connections between some key findings of modern cognitive science and the practical success of our Metaphor Project tools and resources.

By the time you finish this book, you will have learned what you need to know now about how to reach mainstream America: what "speaking American" is, exactly how progressives can do it, and how to answer the holdouts who resist trying it. Most important of all, you'll have learned how to do it yourself. In this age when everyone can be an activist, and social networks move at the speed of light, we can't always wait for the experts to tell us exactly which metaphor category or words to use. We have to step up to the plate ourselves when the moment comes, and make our own moves.

By giving everyone the methods and tools to do smart American Framing, we aim to amp up progressive capacity to meet today's challenges. That is what The Metaphor Project (MP) has been about since day one, back in 1997, when we started up right after a test workshop at a local conference. We hope this book will carry our message about American Framing to many more in the progressive community and help to bring about real change in our country.

Susan C. Strong
for The Metaphor Project

PART I

American Framing Gets America's Ear

CHAPTER 1

Why American Framing
Gets America's Ear

It was American Framing, or "patriotic language," that temporarily unified most of the nation on January 21, 2009, a date that will remain famous in American history, regardless of what came after it. At his historic inauguration as the first African-American head of state, President Obama spoke about the American people's fidelity "to the ideals of our forebears, and [of our being] true to our founding documents." Using the most popular American metaphor, the journey, he called on us to return to the core values that have been "a quiet force of progress throughout our history." The values he cited were "hard work and honesty, courage and fair play, tolerance and curiosity, loyalty and patriotism." He powerfully evoked these values by retelling a core piece of The Ideal American Identity Story—Washington's proclamation to the American people, as he camped with his soldiers by a bitterly cold river. Obama said:

> "At a moment when the outcome of our revolution was most in doubt, the father of our nation ordered these words be read to the people:
>
> > 'Let it be told to the future world that in the depth of winter, when nothing but hope and virtue could survive, that the city and the country, alarmed at one common danger, came forth to meet it.' "

Obama (and his speechwriter) knew that to keep his campaign promises, he would have to reach a very broad section of the electorate: "the persuadables."[1] These are the same moderate Democrats, independents, and moderate conservatives that we also have a reasonable hope of reaching. Of course, there were many listening that day who had no intention of cooperating with Obama. Today a lot of us question his sincerity. But the fact remains that throughout American history, American Framing, or "speaking American," has been the only way to reach and activate large sectors of the public.[2] In the 2008 campaign, Obama's message spoke to the heart of America. The hopes and dreams he evoked are still there, though we are deeply disappointed. The message needs to come from us now, as we organize to pressure our government in more effective ways.

Although "speaking American" is always a feature of "big vision" speeches by politicians, it's ideal for talking about our own vision of what America should be. That's because it has the power to carry our proposals into everyday political discussion. A good example of that is the slogan popularized by Van Jones: "Rebuild the American Dream." We should all be handing our representatives that kind of lively language. Along with the policy details we want them to enact, they need popularly accessible metaphors and phrases for each goal.

"Speaking American" is vital for our grassroots organizing work too. If we are speaking American about what we want, more persuadable folks out there are likely to get our message. The Union of Concerned Scientists provides a good model with their American sound bite for the climate change debate: "Got science?" That's a visceral echo of the original "Got milk?" slogan. It has spawned dozens of progressive variations because of its enormous popular appeal. "Got science?" suggests that today sound science is as vital to our survival as something most people take for granted—milk. We progressives know that's true, but communicating it in a popular sound bite works best.[3]

Speaking American is Progressive

In the last few years a lot has been written and said about progressive values. At first, the challenge was just to decide what such values were and whether we could agree on them. Some implied that progressive values weren't even common American values — they were different and special, found only among progressives and their close sympathizers.

Mercifully, we're past that stage now. The 2008 Obama presidential campaign made it clear that progressive values *are* the best American values. No matter what has happened during his administration since, nothing can take that away from us. We saw that all progressive values are deeply rooted in the story of who Americans are when we are at our best — fair, law-abiding, honest, hard-working, community-minded, cooperative, egalitarian, compassionate, public-spirited, and creative. Because of this change, we progressives can be proud to call ourselves Americans again. No matter what our government or even the nutcases among our people do, we know that we ourselves can speak American with complete integrity.

In fact, being progressive has always been quintessentially American. Renowned pollster Celinda Lake reminded participants at the 2008 Take Back America Conference that as a people we're all about progress. Progressive commentator Thom Hartmann reviewed the origins of modern liberalism and conservatism in his book, *Cracking the Code*, to remind us that, despite their flaws or omissions, our Declaration of Independence and Constitution have a real liberal pedigree.[4]

In *The End of America*, Naomi Wolf says this of our founders: "These men and women...were walking further out into the unknown—betting on ordinary people's capacities—than anyone had ever walked in the history of the human race."[5] At the time our nation began, most European political thinkers believed that monarchy, hopefully an enlightened one, was absolutely necessary for workable human government. Our founders didn't agree and proved those pessimists wrong. True, they were people of property, racists, and patriarchal in their views. But by the way they set up our government (unwittingly, perhaps), they made it possible for progress to keep on happening after they were gone.

For these reasons, the long arc of American history has proven that social change work is most effective when it invokes the model of our best ideals as a nation. That's why Martin Luther King, Jr., ended his famous "I Have a Dream" speech with a series of stirring visions, starting with, "I have a dream that one day this nation will rise up and live out the true meaning of its creed: 'We hold these truths to be self-evident, that all men are created equal.'"[6] It's why the latest struggle for freedom within our country, gay rights, has been rightly framed as a demand for civil rights.

A recent American Framing change reflects this tactic too. Although the preferred progressive framing for undocumented immigrants used to be "undocumented workers," because hard work is still a very important part of The Ideal American Story, lately that has changed.[7] Fear of such migrants taking scarce American jobs has made some immigration rights activists prefer the term "human beings," in order to evoke the even larger American category of "human rights." Another version inspired by the same concern is "undocumented persons."[8]

Experts Agree: Speaking American Works Best

Successful American political consultants know our ideal national story remains the most vital touchstone in our political communication today. Two notable books illustrate this point. In *The True Patriot*, Bill Clinton's speechwriter Eric Liu and his colleague, Nick Hanauer, talk about where they found the language for their work:

> "We simply captured the essence of what America's civic leaders and heroes have been saying for over 200 years. It was through our year of research that we realized that America doesn't need a new politics; it simply needs to reconnect with its *original* patriotic traditions."[9]

Another veteran progressive operative, Bernie Horn, Senior Fellow at the Campaign for America's Future and author of *Framing the*

Future, also demonstrates the absolute necessity of what I call "speaking American."[10] Horn advises progressives to start out by saying we are for such common American values as "freedom, opportunity, and security for all." He also suggests we speak of "community, society, America," or "we," instead of "government."[11] He notes that "tax fairness, fair markets," and "[helping] Main Street" are phrases with real power.[12] I'd add to his remarks that being positive and talking about what you want, not what you dislike, has more power most of the time.

Horn's credibility is high. While Senior Director for Policy and Communications at the Center for Policy Alternatives, he oversaw training and guidance for innumerable winning progressive political candidates, including Senator Jon Tester (Montana), Congressman Keith Ellison (Minnesota), and Congresswoman Gabrielle Giffords (Arizona), among others. His suggestions have been validated by the work of progressive pollster Celinda Lake and by groups such as The FrameWorks Institute and Demos.

Last but not least, from another quarter of the progressive political spectrum comes advice from one of our most famous bloggers. In *Taking On The System*, legendary blogger Markos Moulitsas Zuniga, founder of the important political blog the *Daily Kos*, warns his readers that, "Emotional connection moves us. Statistics do not. Unlike 'facts,' we process values at the gut level, not by using reason."[13] In *Re:Imagining Change*, Patrick Reinsborough and Doyle Canning of SmartMeme make the same point and provide explicit guidance for creating progressive stories that carry real meaning for their own audiences.[14]

Stories make the emotional connection to values, and American story words do it best of all. Here are a few samples from The Metaphor Project's own collection of recommendations:

- ❖ "Choose the 'cool it' option," used when Iran was threatened by the Bush administration with pre-emptive strikes

- Try "course change," recommended in the summer of 2006 and becoming fully mainstream by November of 2006

- "The One Big Family Frame," the title of a Metaphor Project web essay about an important part of the American political story

- "American truth bites," for the American sound bites we often suggest

For more about these and other examples of "speaking American" from The Metaphor Project, see Part II: More American Frames That Stuck.

Speaking American Fluently

The specific words and phrases that Liu, Hanauer, and Horn, recommend convey some important bits of The American Cultural Narrative. Such suggestions are similar to a phrasebook we take with us when traveling in a foreign country—a good thing to have in a pinch, on a short trip. However, if you want to communicate well with mainstream Americans, you need to know how to speak American fluently yourself.

Even when cognitive science researchers have recommended a specific conceptual metaphor formula, such as "the economy is a car we control," it is still up to us to find the language of everyday metaphor that will best evoke that idea for our own audiences.[15] In this case, we need to be able to say things like "we can fix the economy," or "the economy needs some repairs," or "we need to stop driving the economy into the ditch." That's speaking American.

Just like real proficiency in a foreign language, fluency in speaking American makes us independently capable of shaping our own messages. Fortunately, this skill is actually a lot easier to acquire than learning a new language! You already know a lot more about speaking American than you think you do. It's the purpose of this book to show you how to access and use that knowledge effectively.

CHAPTER 2

American Stories You Can Use

The patriotic language President Obama used in his first inaugural speech included common American values like fair play, loyalty, and patriotism. He invoked these classic American themes to give power to his "new story" of where America should head in the coming years. Predictably, the next day the fight began over how to express those values. The trouble always starts the minute we move off the abstract level.

Practical consequences are the sticky wicket, as cognitive scientist George Lakoff demonstrated in his book, *Whose Freedom?*[1] Even a core American value like freedom gets complicated when it comes down to specifics. Lakoff reminds us that conservatives see being free as having no government regulation or taxes. Progressives feel free when government guarantees their privacy, free speech, and other civil rights.[2]

As Howard Fineman shows in *The Thirteen American Arguments*, some of these disputes go back to early American days. They reappear in different forms as the times and issues change.[3] For example, American arguments about equality started with the slavery question. They reappeared in the debate over giving women the vote. Today they manifest as conflict over unborn fetuses or gay rights. But most people still agree that equality as an abstract idea is a core American value.

We progressives must also begin our messages with "patriotic" language: the phrases, images, and metaphors that evoke ideal American values. This is especially important in today's bitterly partisan climate. To be heard at all, we must start with a credible appeal to our nation's ideal identity, phrased in ways that most Americans can hear. When we want to talk about specific actions, the importance of speaking American is even greater. *Our* "new story" about America will work best if it seems to fit a familiar piece of the American story.[4] To get our detailed talking points heard, we must start from the common ground of our shared American identity.

Using The Ideal American Identity Story and The American Cultural Narrative

Before we decide exactly how to phrase our messages, we need to be aware of the different parts of "the American story." The Ideal American Identity Story is a set of uncontested ideas, traits, and values most of us share. It's about who we are as a people when we are at our best. We Americans believe in democracy, the rule of law, opportunity, freedom, and fair play. We progressives accept that story as an expression of our ideals too.

But we also need to be aware of another type of American story. I call it The American Cultural Narrative.[5] It includes some ideal subplots and some less-than-pure mini-narratives, all derived from our nation's historical experience. From a progressive point of view, some parts of this cultural narrative appear unappealing, harmful, or in conflict with each other or with our goals. But all can be useful—in the right setting.[6]

When we choose familiar American phrases, images, and metaphors for our own messages, it's vital to recall which words express which type of story. If we make the right choice of language, we can evoke powerful American ideals and cultural subplots. For example, Robert Reich has long identified four familiar American political subplots.[7] They are "mob at the gates," "rot at the top," "the triumphant individual," and "the benevolent community."

Conservatives are usually more worried about "the mob at the gates" and believe in "the triumphant individual." Progressives tend to be more suspicious of "rot at the top." We feel that social factors heavily condition individual success and believe the solution to our problems lies in creating a more "benevolent community." Of course, if the Democrats are in power, the conservatives will see "rot at the top" in too much government action or spending. (Actual language that evokes these four plots is included in The Metaphor Project's American Story Elements List, also described in this chapter.)

We can recognize Reich's four cultural narratives as they appear in today's politics. Think of the ongoing struggle over immigration policy in Washington, with some people manifesting great fear of the "mob" of Hispanic immigrants "at our gates." Then there's outrage on both sides about the "rot at the top" that has been going on in D.C. and on Wall Street in recent years. In 2008, "triumphant individual" multimillionaire T. Boone Pickens came up with his own personal plan for a natural gas/wind U.S. energy solution.[8] And, of course, we progressives responded powerfully at first to President-Elect Obama's vision of "the benevolent community": post-partisan, problem-solving, and caring.

Reich is one of many scholars who have studied American Cultural Narrative.[9] Writing for the Fetzer Institute's *Essays on Deepening the American Dream* series, Betty Sue Flowers suggests there are four different American stories about our history: a religious myth about our origins and mission, a hero myth about daring individuals who shape the country, a democratic myth that celebrates the rule of law and reason, and today's dominant myth, the one where economics drives everything. Writing for the same Fetzer series, Carol S. Pearson finds there are three pairs of opposing American character types: the explorer vs. the lover, the warrior vs. the caregiver, and the jester vs. the sage.[10]

Of course, there are many more subplots and character types in The American Cultural Narrative. To speak American well, we need to be aware of the full spectrum. When we are reminded of specific elements in these American stories, they seem familiar (even if some seem to contradict others). As members of the same national community, we know them implicitly, whether we like them or not. But if we are learning to speak American fluently, we need more than that. The stories and the language that evokes them need to be at our fingertips.

That's why The Metaphor Project has developed two handy reference lists: The American Story Elements List and The American Metaphor Categories List.[11] These lists of themes and the language that evokes them are meant to be memory teasers. They remind you of what you already know at a deeper level. They also stimulate memories of other items not included in our lists. They are vital tools used in our American Framing Steps. (In Part III I'll show you exactly how to use them all, as part of that process.) Our lists have been developed through an ongoing process of interdisciplinary research and experimentation over many years. The themes they contain are important parts of both The Ideal American Identity Story and The American Cultural Narrative. Favorites of both the Left and the Right are included, because that facilitates a faster, more intuitive American Framing process.[12] Some activists have even found they can make use of American story elements that progressives often reject. An example of this is the way that some fair trade activists have used cartoon or comic book superheroes to help get their point across.

Both lists cover aspects of the American story, but each presents that story in a different way.[13] The American Story Elements List is strictly thematic. The American Metaphor Categories List breaks our cultural narratives down in a different way. It provides more entry points, but less internal linkage. For best results, the lists should be used together as we do in our American Framing Steps.

Right now it will be most useful to start by looking at some general descriptions of The American Story Elements. (We'll go over the actual list along with The American Metaphor Categories List in Chapter 9.) At this point it's more important to get a quick thematic overview of the American story in all of its many forms.

The American Story Elements List includes the following seven categories:

1. The American Dream
2. The American Nation
3. Free to Succeed
4. We're on a Roll
5. Small Town Security
6. Man to Superman
7. The American Nightmare

1. The American Dream

The most important element of The American Cultural Narrative is The American Dream. Although today that phrase is often narrowed to the dreams of our current consumer culture, there is a larger American dream still alive in our country. It is the dream of a better country and of a better world. This more inclusive American dream is based on the feeling that we are the "can do" people, who can turn on a dime to do the impossible better than anyone else. We are the pioneering people, who are always on the frontier of the new. We look to the future, we're optimistic, and we do what works. When we make mistakes, we redeem, restore, renew, or reinvent ourselves. We like things to be bigger, better, higher, and fresher. We are a problem-solving people.

The next story element expresses another aspect of the ideal American national dream.

2. The American Nation

This story element conveys our ideals about our country. We are a new kind of nation, a beacon of hope for the world, the cradle and home of political freedom, democracy's defender and champion, the home of equal opportunity and of the rule of law. As a nation, we dream of being fair to all, and we are willing to try new ways to solve the world's problems. We protect human and civil rights. In this ideal version, we see ourselves as a classless society. We also see ourselves as being a melting pot nation.

An important reason we like to see ourselves as a classless society relates to another American story element.

3. Free to Succeed

A big part of the individual's dream in America is the idea that here barriers to personal success do not exist, if people work hard enough. Owning your own home or business is seen as a reasonable goal. If you're lucky, yours will be a "rags to riches" story too, like the famous Horatio Alger, our archetypal triumphant individual. Moreover, if you do succeed, it will be the product of your own talent, personal virtue, and hard work alone. It will not be because of luck, your social status, or connections. (Americans have a big blind spot about the role of social or physical infrastructure in helping the individual succeed.) Competition is seen as healthy and as bringing out the best in people. Everyone is supposed to want to be a winner or be on the winning team. And in our country, winning is often expressed by the next element.

4. We're on a Roll

This story element is what's behind the American idea that a rising tide automatically lifts all boats. It also expresses the most common all-around American metaphor—being in motion of some kind. Some of the other language that conveys this includes the following: going, moving, moving forward, driving, rolling, accelerating, going toward, going at a fast pace, being in the fast lane or on the fast track, going online, taking a trip, traveling, making a journey, escaping, going into action, charging ahead, and being on the move. Naturally, all of this motion can take advantage of every form of vehicle you can think of, from feet to spacecraft.

And as the cushy interiors featured in our car ads show, we want to take the comforts of home with us when we travel. Those comforts of home cover a lot of ground, as the next story element shows.

5. Small Town Security

This story element reflects a different side of the American character and its aspirations. It expresses our nostalgic dream of the ideal small town or community, where everything is clean, safe, moral, friendly, and caring. It's a place where things are orderly and common sense prevails. There you can count on a fair hearing. It's middle America, Main Street, and Reich's benevolent community. Our hope for a wise and farsighted bipartisan consensus lives there.

An important variation of this story element is the "Us vs. Them" mini-narrative. This is the tale of the benevolent grassroots community supporting those who fight to make the ideal American promise come true. Some "Us vs. Them" stories tell about the way workers or slaves have successfully pushed back against oppression by owners. Others are about the way the poor and immigrants have prevailed in struggles with the rich. Then there are the "Us vs. Them" stories about modern people of color standing up to dominant whites.

These "Us vs. Them" mini-narratives break the conventional American taboo against admitting that class or race matter in America. But the solutions they offer rely on important aspects of The Ideal American Identity Story: "can do" traits and American ideals of fairness, equality, and opportunity.

Right alongside these "Us vs. Them" subplots is another important piece of our national mythology about what rights the wrongs of our society.

6. Man to Superman

The "Man to Superman" element reflects a common theme in American popular culture. It's about the superhuman man, woman, or child who comes to rescue people, cities, or countries, sometimes even the world. Familiar examples include the cowboy, the sheriff, Clark Kent/Superman (U.S. presidents are often compared to Superman), Spiderman, Catwoman, and Superwoman. Variations on the theme come from the world of science: Batman, Lara Croft, James Bond, MacGyver, and Iron Man. These are the tech-fix saviors. Today's superseeds and supergenes are non-human versions of those superfolk. Superheroes save us from the next story element.

7. The American Nightmare

The American Nightmare has many aspects. Beyond the fear of terrorism, immigrants, and war, people often see danger coming from the government. On the Left, the "too much" category includes secrecy, deception, lies, conspiracy, secret deals, violation of rights, of freedom, or of the rule of law. Cheating the public and betraying the public trust go in this category too.

Many Americans also fear taxes and spending—breaking the budget. Then there's government control in the form of regulation. Of course, "rot at the top" may also be a corrupt connection between business and government, or within the world of business. Racism and discrimination are forms of rot too.

"Going too far" in any direction scares most Americans. Some people also fear limits to U.S. sovereignty through the jurisdiction of the World Court, international treaties, the U.N., or other international bodies.

American Story Elements Persist

As you read through the above paragraphs, you may have said to yourself, "I knew all of that!" Of course you do. There are many modern studies that document the remarkable staying power of basic American cultural values and themes.[14] Scholars agree that, barring cataclysmic events, change in social norms (or the words that evoke them) usually occurs only on the surface of a society.[15] We also know it from our own experience. For example, the freewheeling 1990's seemed to shift suddenly to the extremely security-conscious 2000's after 9/11. But being security-conscious was already a strong American trait before 9/11. The crisis merely brought that reality to the fore in a powerful new way.

Even then, there were many well-documented areas of American life where the "can do," "try something new" spirit remained very much alive—alternative energy initiatives, to take just one example. More recently, the explosion of the Web 2.0 world and the rise of social networking reflect these traits.

Why Some Progressives Haven't Used What They Already Know About Speaking American

There are a variety of reasons why some progressives haven't used what they already know about speaking American. We'll take up some of the most common ones in the next chapter. But we need to notice two important ones right now. First, some progressives haven't done it precisely because that knowledge has been implicit and not conscious.

Second, they haven't known how to use what they know. At the initial Metaphor Project workshop in November 1997, I described the experiment we were going to try. Together we would come up with mainstream-accessible language for environmental sustainability. As we began, many of the participants thought they couldn't do it. So we began by brainstorming a simple list of some familiar American cultural themes like the cowboy story, the mafia story, and the melting pot nation idea.

As the list grew, participants began to understand that they actually did know both The Ideal American Identity Story and The American Cultural Narrative. The next step, using this material to create just the right mainstream-accessible language, began to look like fun. People started to see how speaking American could work to carry progressive messages. Results of our early workshops are still available on The Metaphor Project website in the Examples section. They are also included in Appendix II of this book. Some of those results are still usable—phrases like the "we generation," "eco-centric," "lean and green," and "solar security," among others.

As time went on, we were able to validate these early workshop experiments through a program of ongoing research and testing. Combining their format with widely accepted rules for fostering good communication, we developed our current set of American Framing Steps, tools, and resources. Today these resources can help you recall what you already know, and guide you in creating smarter messages. They can also ensure that you avoid "tin ear" (tone deaf) results from an unsystematic, hit-or-miss framing process.

CHAPTER 3

More Answers for Critics, Rebels, and the Confused

At the end of Chapter 2, we looked at two important reasons some progressives haven't been speaking American: they aren't aware of how important it is, and they don't realize they actually know something about how to do it. But other progressives actively object to the idea of speaking American. Next we'll look at ways to answer their arguments, from the simplest to the most comprehensive.

The most common objections to speaking American include:

1. Rejection of any kind of persuasion deemed too feeling-based or deliberate

2. Refusal to use anything that looks like a tagline, cliché, or sound bite

3. Belief that we need a totally "new" story that avoids any existing American story elements

4. Rejection of anything that sounds like it could be related in any way to "American exceptionalism"

5. Reaction against the Right's cooptation of ideal American story language

6. Anger about longstanding American hypocrisy in relation to our ideals

7. Fear that "speaking American" is "talking white"

We'll look at each of these concerns in the order given above. While none are good reasons to avoid speaking American, it's important to give them a serious look.

1. Rejection of Any Kind of Persuasion Deemed Too Feeling-Based or Deliberate

Despite my efforts and those of Professors George Lakoff and Drew Westen, some progressives still believe in using purely intellectual arguments. They prefer to rely on reasons, facts, and statistics alone. But Lakoff and Westen have both written at length about the scientific fact that storytelling works best.[1] They have proven that people ignore talking points packed with facts and statistics, if those facts and statistics don't match the stories in their own heads. So why do some progressives still prefer to use the fact/stat mode?

Foremost, perhaps, is the fact that for some progressives, reasons, facts, statistics, and history do *appear* to work more persuasively.[2] As a group, many of us on the Left believe we process political information in a different way than most people in our country. We like to think we can only be persuaded by facts or scientific proof. One reason for this stance may be that a strong suspicion of emotion has dominated intellectual life in modern society—both in the U.S. and abroad—for several centuries. This situation has only recently been successfully challenged in the public mind by the work of Daniel Goleman, author of *Emotional Intelligence*.[3]

In fact, contemporary cognitive science demonstrates that in reality persuasion occurs the same way for us all. We make decisions about what to believe long before we become conscious of having done so. We all go through the same unconscious process of mixed feeling and reasoning that George Lakoff has dubbed "real reason."[4] As he has shown, powerful moral feelings motivate us all. Facts and scientific proof just add more weight to a prior decision-making process. And it's very well-documented that moral feelings are best evoked by story.[5]

These facts suggest that if we progressives want our vision of a better world to come true, we need to pay more attention to what works for the general public. To get the best possible results, we would be wise to translate our message into colorful, story-evoking language or images. If we really care about our issues, we'll make the effort to persuade others in the most effective way.

However, another thread of the "rational" critique says we should deliberately communicate in a more elevated and original way with the public, avoiding all popular clichés, metaphors, and images. Proponents of this view feel that doing so would improve the quality of the public's thinking. Unfortunately, critical thinking must be taught in school—not in the heat of political battle. This is especially true now, as conservatives have perfected the art of simple and deceptive narrative communication. Today, they spread their lies everywhere by means of their extensive media network. It's time more of us fought back in equally effective ways.

The last variation on this type of objection is actually strongly feeling-based. Some people who resist speaking American or even trying to use story-based language feel they are protecting their own integrity by adopting this stance. The "integrity" objection usually boils down to a feeling that if we do anything at all to adjust our communication style to persuade our audiences, we are being dishonest or unfairly manipulative.

I propose a much more progressive way to look at this. If we make an effort to communicate in a way that people understand, we demonstrate the progressive values of empathy and responsibility. We can keep our integrity intact when we talk about how Americans can better embody ideal American values. It's deeply considerate and kind to speak to people in ways they understand. We should be taking the responsibility to reach out to them this way.

2. Refusal to Use or Create "Simplistic" Taglines, Sound Bites, or Clichés

Some progressives don't want to speak American because they know it can mean using familiar catch phrases, clichés, and political metaphors. They have watched the Right misuse sound bites in order to manipulate for years. It's no wonder some recoil.

But, as a friend of mine says, "Using a perfectly good shovel as a murder weapon doesn't make it a bad tool for planting a garden." It's true that you can't pack a lot of nuanced talking points into a sound bite. But sound bites are good tools for getting people's attention in the first place. We might even think of sound bites as "seeds" we're planting—small, compact openers. We can use sound bites ourselves and keep our integrity, because ours can be the trenchant American "truth bites" that finally bring an issue into the open.[6] Only then will there be an audience for our talking points and the nuances they may express.

Chip and Dan Heath, authors of *Made to Stick,* have a great way of describing the kind of sound bite we want to use: "Proverbs are sound bites that are profound."[7] In a chapter of *Rules for Radicals* called "A Word about Words," Saul Alinsky cited Mark Twain this way: "The difference between the right word and the almost right word is the difference between lightning and the lightning bug."[8] Tagline guru Eric Swartz says, "A good tagline connects with your audience at the emotional level."[9]

Today, experts say we have 15 seconds or less to get the public's attention. That's why the sound bite is such an essential item in politics. Unless we happen to be a major political figure giving a prime time political speech, we operate under this constraint. Even skilled orators lose in the end if they don't deploy the right sound bites at the right time. As former President Bill Clinton once exclaimed: "...we can litanize and analyze all we want, but until people can say it in a phrase, we're sunk."[10] Our phrases had better be memorable enough to stick in people's minds.

Jonathan Alter described this phenomenon in a brilliant 2008 *Newsweek* piece on the subject, entitled "I'm Rubber, You're Glue":

> "...memorable lines, images, gaffes and monikers are like a piece of gum on the bottom of your shoe. They get your attention and may even shape your voting behavior. In the world of marketing, 'sticky branding' means intentionally creating an emotional attachment."[11]

He goes on to say that [in politics] it's vital to find "the quirky expression or colorful figure of speech that someone might actually remember." He also points out that "the most common standard for stickiness is whether it fits into a pre-existing impression." This stickiness factor is the rock bottom reason why we progressives need to express our messages using colorful metaphors.

Even the new prominence of video clips on YouTube or tweets on Twitter has not altered this situation. After all, it's the catchy headline, subject line, tweet, or text message that best spreads the word about what's hot on YouTube. AlterNet Executive Editor Don Hazen points out that "headlines, subject lines and teasers are the most powerful and visible communication tools to connect immediately with readers."[12]

Of course, most mainstream Americans still get the majority of their political information from television, where sound bites have been king for decades. Sound bites may be the only way we're going to get any version of our own message before the vast American TV audience. We need something "sticky" enough to at least open the door for questions when the set is turned off. That means something that sounds somewhat familiar, but with a lively kicker.

This point brings up the next objection—the feeling some progressives have that we need a totally new story, one that avoids any elements of the old American story.

3. The Belief that We Need a Totally "New" Story

Sometimes outraged progressives say we need a brand new story because The Ideal American Identity Story is a complete lie. Always looking for something new is actually a core American value—a quintessential part of the ideal American identity. So there's something quite endearing about this group of critics. But we need to avoid throwing the true American baby out along with the phony American bath water.

We know that there is always a contemporary "battle of the story" going on, as the group SmartMeme puts it.[13] The battle usually has two levels. Both get expressed in the struggle between contemporary "instrumental stories." (An instrumental story is about what works to get what people want now.) A good example of both levels of story battle is the neocon narrative about "free markets" and "free trade" that has dominated our economic life since the Reagan era. The free market story has two major and distinct components: the myth that the market knows best and should be left completely unregulated, and the way the word "free" works in the story. The ideal American identity word "free" is used to foster the idea that this behavior is the right way for Americans to do things.

The free trade policy itself is presented as being the only practical way to create prosperity, which is false. Attaching the ideal American value word "free" to the story is also deceptive. But being "free" is a genuine and worthy American value by itself. That's the American baby we want to keep.

Progressives usually counter the "free market story" with the "fair market story" where "fair trade" and adequate regulation guarantee that everyone gets what they need, not just the few. The progressive market story evokes another ideal American value: fairness. Today, progressive versions of the market story may be gaining ground, as the flaws of "free markets" and "free trade" start to bite us harder.

In every battle over what the true instrumental story is, skillful application of the right American story language is essential for society-wide change. This fact has never been more important to understand than it is today, as the epic battle over framing government, taxes, and budgets continues to rage. Shaping a new and better instrumental story about any topic is the first step in any "battle of the story."[14] But framing it for maximum effectiveness means using powerful American identity words, like fair rules, honest reporting, socially responsible democracy, or public safety.

The importance of framing in this kind of fight has been verified by decades of communication studies.

A good example of how to do this task well comes from a notable effort to make the American lifestyle more ecologically sustainable. I'm thinking of the Democracy School, which teaches people to assert their "community rights" against polluting corporations. They have combined two classic American themes, "community" and "rights," to create an instantly familiar American idea. Another good model of speaking American about the move to sustainability comes from the Blue-Green Alliance. They call for "clean energy jobs." Americans love to have things "clean" and right now especially, "a clean job" has double appeal. It's also part of creating "new" industries, another typical American theme—"renewing" or "reinventing" American manufacturing.[15]

A different kind of American story some progressives automatically reject is also a big piece of The American Cultural Narrative: the story some American sports metaphors tell. This is understandable, given the progressive commitment to increasing social and economic justice. The idea that everything should be decided by competition alone ignores the social and economic barriers that prevent an equal basis for competition. Competition as a litmus test for what people deserve also promotes an uncaring, uncooperative idea of how a society should work.

However, not all sports metaphors work this way. "Play by the rules" provides a good example of the way the American love of sports can work in our favor. It promotes a visceral grasp of one vital principle of our democracy—the rule of law. "Play fair," and "be a good sport" also express values progressives can support. Because so many Americans understand and accept sports ethics, we progressives need to be able to use appropriate sports metaphors ourselves.

However, the idea that we need a totally new story sometimes comes in a different form.

4. Rejection of Anything that Sounds Like "American Exceptionalism"

Another very important thread in some progressives' resistance to speaking American is linked to rejecting anything that seems like "American exceptionalism."[16] That's the idea that America is better and more moral than all other nations. It also includes the assumption that our country has a God-given historical mission to fulfill on the global scene. Certainly, when the idea of our specialness as a democracy is used to exploit others through force, it's a lie that creates a nightmare. Worse, many politicians and members of the public don't seem to recognize the nightmare version for what it really is until after the fact, if ever. Outrages such as the Iraq War or the continuing Afghan conflict are sold to the public as part of our historical destiny to bring democracy to everyone else. Too many can't seem to distinguish between ideal versions of our national identity and absolute violations of it.

However, as I have been arguing throughout this book, we can't afford to drop a useful tool like speaking American just because it's abused by someone else. We must use it to fight the corruption that American exceptionalism can foster. Even Professor Bacevich, author of *The Limits of Power: The End of American Exceptionalism*, speaks about some important ideal American values when he writes the following:

> "A realistic appreciation of limits, on the other hand, creates opportunities to adjust policies and replenish resources — perhaps even to renew institutions. Constraints subject old verities to reconsideration, promote fresh thinking, and unleash creativity."[17]

In a 2010 *New York Review of Books* article, Geoffrey Wheatcroft points to an American tradition of pragmatism, practicality, and hostility to foreign wars, entangling alliances, and "meddling in distant countries."[18] Johan Galtung, founding father of peace studies, urges us to "hate the American empire," but "love the American republic, just as so many people all over the world do."[19]

Throughout American history, reformers have called the nation to a higher standard of behavior by invoking parts of our ideal identity story. Now more than ever, we must use its power to check our government's behavior. The current economic crisis offers us unique opportunities to do this. The need for "limits" is built in, and the focus can be on "reinventing" America in a way that works now.

More evidence for this view comes from some bona fide citizens of the world. I once heard Martin Khor, former director of the Third World Network, now executive director of the South Center in Geneva—an internationalist by profession—say that the most important thing Americans can do about the world's problems is to change American behavior. Calling on positive traits that Americans idealize is the only way we can do this with success.

A striking example of how this works comes from Warren Buffet. He famously advised Bono in his effort to get more American aid for Africa as follows: "Appeal to American greatness, not American conscience."[20] "American greatness" can be interpreted as our ability to face and solve problems in practical, innovative ways. Buffet's advice sheds light on how best to meet our current problems. Invoking our ideal national identity is the way to get Americans moving. Speaking American is the key to doing that.

5. Reacting to the Right's American Story Cooptation

Clearly, in the last few decades, conservatives have used many elements of The Ideal American Identity Story to lie about what they were really doing. Linguistic historian Geoffrey Nunberg has documented the ways this happened in his book, *Talking Right.*[21] G.W. Bush era deceptions like "no child left behind" and "clear skies" are just a few examples of this "Machiavellian" language.[22] As a result, some American progressives have become violently allergic to any colorful language that evokes The Ideal American Identity Story. In their minds, every example of that type of framing now risks being seen as equally dishonest.

But the Right has been outframing us since the Reagan era, and the country has been going further downhill every year. We need to get off our high horse and get serious about more effective communication ourselves. It's our patriotic duty. Moreover, our future depends on our sharpening up and speaking American about our own messages. Speaking American works for the Right exactly because Americans want to be as good as their ideal national identity story suggests. We need to make this desire work in our favor.

6. Anger about Longstanding American Hypocrisy

Of course, hypocritical behavior by our government is not a recent thing. We've seen a lot of it over the long sweep of American history, from initial contradictions in our founding documents to recurrent betrayal of our ideals. These problems have led some progressives to completely reject The Ideal American Identity Story as a source of persuasive framing. They feel that any form of speaking American is merely a case of using the oppressor's lying language. They fear it will just feed American delusions about who we are and what we do.

All too often, however, if we are talking to the public, this kind of progressive alienation actually deprives us of the very tools we need to fight back. To move ahead successfully, we must call on the American people and our government to fulfil the promise of our best national ideals. We got a start on this with the successful 2008 Obama presidential campaign. That opening still exists, and it may even be bigger now. If we progressives and liberals consistently speak American ourselves, we may be able to help create a much deeper national transformation over the long haul.

7. Fear that "Speaking American" is "Talking White"

Although I've already covered many forms of rebellion against the idea of speaking American, there's one more. It's also generated by anger about a special form of American hypocrisy. People of color are often fighting mad about not receiving what America seems to promise. They see the white elite systematically frustrating their attempts to get ahead. So they may assume that if we recommend speaking American, it's because we think they should "talk white."

All organizers know they must use language current within their own communities to organize their base. But when communities of color want to push any level of government or the mainstream public for real change, speaking American helps. It's just a way to translate your own message into widely understood story formats via familiar words and metaphors. Organizers can set up this way of communicating long before the crunch. Instead of talking about "speaking American," they can just start doing it. For example, they can urge people to organize for a country in which there is "equal opportunity for all." Van Jones is especially adept at doing it this way.

People who have lived in this country for a while usually know the stories that go with that language. If they are too new to recognize them, others who have lived here longer can help. A good example of how that "translation" process can work comes from the 2006 demonstrations held by undocumented workers demanding immigration reform. One large march started out with march leaders defiantly carrying the Mexican flag. Immediately, they received hysterically negative mainstream American press. But fortunately, someone swiftly gave them the right clue. By the very next day their march leaders were carrying American flags. That was the real point anyway—they are already here working and very often paying American taxes. They deserve to be treated like contributing Americans.

This kind of translation to a "speaking American" approach is also the one taken by the immigrant-focused organization OneAmerica. At one point in the spring of 2010 they quoted Langston Hughes' great poem, *Let America Be America Again*, on their website. They also exemplify what *YES! Magazine* called "America: The Remix" on its Spring 2010 cover.[23] The very clever "remix" metaphor is a wonderful example of speaking American. The young and iTunes-savvy will get this reference immediately. It's also about a uniquely American metaphor almost everyone knows well: the American melting pot that freely mixes everything together to create something new.

The Exception that Proves the Rule

Despite the importance of speaking American when addressing the general public, there is one exception. If you are organizing an ethnic base that still communicates in its original language, such as the Asian-American populations of San Francisco, you will need to find matching stories, metaphors, images, and catch phrases common in those languages. As organizers of the California 2009 anti-Proposition 23 Campaign discovered, non-unionized workers in that population actually shared the same values as English-speaking unionized workers. They all cared about protecting the state's new sustainable energy law.[24] (Proposition 23 would have invalidated the new law.) So organizers found Asian phrases that carried the story of those shared values. Prop 23 suffered a very well-deserved defeat, and those Asian-American voters were an important part of that success.

This example demonstrates what I mean when I say the exception proves the rule. To evoke shared values we need stories, and to convey stories quickly we need to use the familiar cultural language that reminds people of them. In America, most of the time, that means speaking American. But The Metaphor Project's general model can be adapted to activate the most powerful cultural or sub-cultural metaphors in any political situation.

What's Next

I hope this survey of how to answer some common objections to speaking American will help you persuade others. In Parts II and III of this book, you'll find additional tools for that job. Part II contains Metaphor Project examples of successful American Framing. Part III explains exactly how to use our American Framing Steps to "speak American." Part III also reveals the secret ingredient of our process.

But before we go on to what follows, it's important to look at one particular way we humans use or create new language. The Metaphor Project's American Framing Steps simply heighten and focus natural abilities we all have. We'll look next at what a lucky few have done all by themselves. That will help us get a sense of what's possible for any of us, when we have the right methods, tools, and resources.

CHAPTER 4

Some Mighty Metaphors
and How They Happened

Most experts on communication agree that metaphor is the master key to political persuasion—the most powerful and efficient way to connect two different ideas. A good metaphor also conveys a complete story in a few words. Cognitive scientist George Lakoff often cites a painful example of this fact: the Right-wing phrase, "tax relief."

Here, the idea of taxes—never a charming thought for Americans—is tied to the idea of "relief." The most common use of the word "relief" in American popular culture is "pain relief," a phrase used to advertise over-the-counter painkillers. The "tax relief" metaphor makes a tax cut seem like a harmless aspirin. It will free you personally from an almost physical pain. (Never mind the pain we'll all feel later, after we've cut vital public services.) Ever since the Reagan era this little metaphor, "tax relief," has done huge damage to our country. How does this trick work? It gets its power from the way metaphor is created and understood in the human brain; it arises in the same location as the physical experience evoked.[1] In this case, "tax relief" literally gets read as relief from physical pain.

The power of metaphor to convey a story in a visceral way also allows it to suggest follow-up action. Another unhappy example of this comes from the aftermath of 9/11. I'm talking about the national debate about how to frame 9/11: Was it an act of war, a crime, or the symptom of a disease? The choice of metaphor category is always a choice about what story to believe and what action to take.

In the case of 9/11, the Bush administration's deliberate choice of the war metaphor has carried fateful consequences. The framing of 9/11 as an act of war has led us to the "war on terror" and to full-scale war in Afghanistan and Iraq. In addition, the choice of this metaphor category has been the excuse for undermining American constitutional safeguards.

How Some Progressive Political Metaphors Have Moved America

In September 2001, few were able to challenge the war metaphor for 9/11 with success. Prior to that point, only a small number of progressive activists and scholars had even thought about political language this way. Fortunately, that situation has changed.[2] But we progressives still have much room for improvement! This chapter shows how some lucky activists have, by chance, created powerful new metaphors to promote their ideas. In what follows we will explore their natural process and results. This will help us understand why The Metaphor Project's American Framing Steps can help anyone do this too.

Good Ears and Lucky Hits

All human beings have the ability to create new language spontaneously. Leslie Savan's book, *Slam Dunks and No Brainers*, traces the way new American popular language keeps appearing in the U.S. At the beginning of her book, she tells the story of an old man living today in a small village in Senegal. He complained that he couldn't understand what the young men of his village were saying. They were constantly making up new words or using the old ones in new ways.[3] Sound familiar? We Americans have been doing it for a long time, as linguistic historian Geoffrey Nunberg documents in his many publications.[4] All it takes is a good ear and good luck.

We'll look next at four stories of American progressives who "accidentally" created powerful new language. Our four case studies include some pretty well-known progressive phrases: "frankenfood," "buffalo commons," "random acts of kindness," and a surprising success with *TIME* magazine.

The Frankenfood Saga

The "frankenfood" story is highly typical. It reflects the fact that its creator was hopping mad—a common thread in creation stories about new progressive language. The creator of the term "frankenfood" was a professor of English, Paul Lewis. He had been feeling very upset by the genetically modified food problem. On June 2, 1992, he wrote a Letter to the Editor of *The New York Times* (published June 16). In a moment of inspiration, he used the phrase "frankenfood" to describe food altered by genetic modification.

Fortunately, the 19th century novel *Frankenstein* has been repeatedly made into popular movies. The idea of an unnaturally pasted-together being was common knowledge. Merging "Franken" with "food" created an instantly nauseating effect. The new word quickly went viral. It passed into common currency and spawned many other variations, such as "frankenfish" and "frankenforests." By August 13, 2000, William Safire of *The New York Times* had found "franken" used as a prefix for -seeds, -chicken, -pigs, -veggies, -science, and -farmers. Today, this process is by no means over. An interesting mutation is "frankenstate," used by Claire Hope Cummings. She titled her May 2, 2008 *Dissent* magazine article, "Artificial Foods and Corporate Crops: Can We Escape the Frankenstate?"[5] "Frankenbugs" was not far behind; it has been used to describe antibiotic-resistant super germs like MRSA. It's also been applied to insects modified to be sterile. The latest new reference I've seen to that term was on May 20th, 2010, when *The Economist* referred to "frankenbugs" in an article about some completely artificial life forms created by biologist Craig Venter and his colleagues.

The "franken-" phenomenon demonstrates a lot more than the good ear and good luck of the one man who started it all. It reflects the way a whole community can manifest linguistic creativity together. Everyone can get into the act, tweaking the new metaphor, and generating more and more new versions.

Buffalo Commons—Still on the Move

An equally spontaneous inspiration gave rise to the phrase "buffalo commons." This is a highly controversial, extremely mediagenic metaphor. It was first used to name a proposal for restoring the American prairie. In the spring of 1987, two professors, Deborah and Frank Popper, were driving home from a conference about our rapidly depopulating Great Plains. They had been having trouble persuading people that the solution was to have the government buy up and restore large areas of the newly vacant prairie. Their idea was to bring back the native grass and the buffalo to eat it. In the car, they began to discuss the various ways of talking about their proposal. Irritated, one said, "Oh, let's just call it a commons." The other replied, "Let's just give it back to the buffalo."[6] An instant later came a moment of simultaneous creation: together they exclaimed, "buffalo commons."

However, the good professors still didn't know what they had. After they used the phrase in some conversation with journalists from western states, the metaphor took off. Ultimately, the term acted as an enormously powerful educational tool for raising the issues, whether people agreed with the concept or not. Though a "buffalo commons" still has not been implemented as a federal program or park, the idea remains very much alive at the state level. A 2000 State of Montana economic development report included the idea as a possible tourist attraction. In the June 8, 2008 Travel Section of *The New York Times*, Joshua Kurlantzick traced the burgeoning new phenomenon of American prairie eco-tourism right back to the Poppers' "buffalo commons" idea. In November 2009, *The Kansas City Star* supported the idea of a buffalo commons park.

Another recent mention occurred in the Winter 2009 issue of *YES! Magazine*, in an article titled "Life Reclaimed." [7] Jarid Manos, founder of the Great Plains Restoration Council, recounts the way the buffalo commons idea inspired him. He created a nonprofit organization that heals both people and prairie. Today he recruits youth from the inner city and Indian reservations to work on prairie restoration. The latest reference I've found to this metaphor appeared in the title of the 2010 Buffalo Commons Storytelling Festival, based in McCook, Kansas. (Stay tuned for an even bigger comeback of the "buffalo commons" phrase as private bison ranching expands across the Great Plains.)

So why did this metaphor work so well? The phrase "buffalo commons" calls up a familiar image in a surprising context. It combines the two to create a powerful new metaphor. First comes that most American of animals, the buffalo. Next comes the word "commons" — not an image we associate with buffalo! The surprise of it attracts people's attention, as this thumbnail history shows. The original phrase surprised its authors, too. A good political metaphor often gives a sense of the "new" that articulates the intuitively true.

Random Kindness Pays It Forward

The widely known phrase, "Random kindness and senseless acts of beauty," presents an even more dramatic case. Originally, Berkeley peace activist Ann Herbert scribbled the phrase on a placemat during a conversation with her friend, Margaret Paloma Pavel, back in 1982.[8] They wanted to overcome their growing distress about the "random violence of war [with its] senseless acts of cruelty." They felt American society needed an antidote to increasing brutalization. They hoped the new phrase would create a healing counter-movement. Starting with a photocopied booklet explaining what they meant, they began to see growing interest in their work. Finally, a *San Francisco Chronicle* journalist, Adair Lara, heard of the phrase and wrote an article on it for *Glamour*. At that point, the phrase went mainstream, eventually getting the attention of Oprah. In 1993, Herbert and Pavel published *Random Kindness and Senseless Acts of Beauty*, with beautiful illustrations by Mayumi Oda.[9]

Inevitably, the language mutation process also kicked in. It led to another version of the phrase: "random acts of kindness." The idea of "random kindness" was even a source for the 2000 Hollywood film, *Pay It Forward*.[10] Every version of this idea evokes a beloved part of The Ideal American Identity Story—the dream of a small town where everyone cares. The unusual pairing of "random" with kindness and "senseless" with "beauty" were dramatic and new. It worked the way every novel phase does—creating a completely new idea from two previously unrelated parts.

Gulliver Wins Media Notice

At times, one of our progressive metaphors even gets picked up by a presumably hostile corporate media source. Juliette Beck had this experience in 2001, when she was organizing against the exploitative FTAA treaty (Free Trade Area of the Americas). She was being interviewed by *TIME*. They asked her why she thought organizing public protests could stop the treaty. In answer, she spontaneously referred to the well-known story of Gulliver tied up by the Lilliputians. To her surprise, *TIME* printed her exact reply.[11] But it's not really surprising when you think about it. Right then she was speaking the media's (and the public's) real language: metaphor. Her reference to the Lilliputians successfully tying Gulliver up evoked a well-known image. And her "off the cuff" application of it to street demonstrators was a brand new analogy *TIME* just couldn't resist.

Why These Examples Happened and How We Can Do It Too

All of the examples I've cited in this chapter were happy accidents, products of the way our brains naturally function. Modern cognitive science has shown that most of our thinking is unconscious, an intricate blend of feeling and simple forms of unconscious reasoning. The research also documents the way our brains swiftly come up with ideas and language for any situation, a phenomenon some call "rapid cognition."[12] The process relies heavily on metaphor for sorting new things into familiar categories. For example, this is what "frankenfood" does: food is rerouted into the night-mare/unnatural category, which gives us a palpable shock. This type of sorting process goes much faster than any form of deliberate, conscious thinking. (And a good thing it does, too—we probably wouldn't still be around as a species if we hadn't been able to do this.) This is also the way most Americans think about politics when they are getting ready to make a political decision.

Our four case studies show a few activists spontaneously "lucking out" with their language creations. But with the right preparation, resources, and process, we can all produce reliably good results. It's definitely possible to get beyond just hoping luck will strike!

That's why The Metaphor Project's American Framing Steps offer such a breakthrough method. If we want to reach Americans where they are, we need to start by getting in sync with them, cognitively and emotionally. Our method and resources help activists do that. Over the years, they have helped many progressives find the American story language they needed.

In Part III of this book, we'll go into the nuts and bolts of how to do American Framing. But first I want to give you more of a feeling for what American Framing is and how it can be used. In Part II, coming up next, you'll find many Metaphor Project examples of speaking American about political issues.

PART II

More American Frames That Stuck

Introduction to PART II

This introduction reviews a few of The Metaphor Project's most popular American Framing suggestions. These frames spread widely online and sparked change. You'll find the complete web essays that introduced them in Chapters 5–8. A selection of other Metaphor Project (MP) web essays on language make up the rest of Part II.

All of the web essays in Part II were sent to members of our national and international Metaphor Project Network. Our MP Network members include grassroots progressives, nonprofit leaders and staff, Democratic Party leaders, funders, and political consultants, among others. If our Network members like an essay, they often forward it to their own networks. Since 2001, when we first went online, The Metaphor Project has been a web phenomenon, long before blogs or RSS feeds took off. Today we have very solid evidence that our MP Network forms a real "six degrees of connection" multiplier.[1] Our web essays have also been posted online on *Common Dreams, AlterNet, OpEdNews,* and in my diary on the *Daily Kos,* as well as republished in a variety of print sources. The full Metaphor Project archive is available on our website, under the Examples link at *www.metaphorproject.org.*

9/11 and the American Peace Movement

In this part of the book, I've promised to share how some of our American frames came into being, and what effects they had. One of the most dramatic examples of deliberate American Framing I have ever seen occurred in the immediate aftermath of 9/11. It's the story of a young progressive leader who put our American Framing Steps to good use.

This story starts with big missteps by others. The press was anxious to know what peace movement leaders would say about the 9/11 attack immediately after the event. Unfortunately, some of those quoted came across as far out of sync with the public mood. While the ashes were still hot in New York City, and the public still in shock, some chose to talk about how the bombings were "just about oil." While they may have said more than that, those remarks were the ones the media quoted.

Nothing could have been worse for the reputation of the peace movement. Moreover, talking about oil right then only increased the public's fear. People in our country depended on oil to get to their jobs, to take their children to schools or doctors, to heat their houses, and to cook their food. At that time in 2001 there had been no serious media coverage about the need to reduce our oil dependency. There were no real political proposals for making it happen. Global warming was not even a widely accepted problem at that time. The "just about oil" message was a complete disaster for those progressives who used it.

Fortunately, that isn't the only story about a peace movement leader contacted by the media at that time. Peter Ferenbach, at the time Executive Director of California Peace Action, had recently taken a Metaphor Project workshop. Invited to be a spokesperson on the PBS NewsHour the following Monday, he spoke eloquently about the trauma the American people had experienced. Then he pointed out the extreme importance of responding to the attack in the right way. He called for actions that would be clearly consistent with the best American values, the ones we all share.

Peter understood that his audience was the mainstream public. He acknowledged the public's feelings right at the beginning of his message. He knew they were all still in shock from the attack. He understood that their first reaction was likely to be fear and anger, along with a desire for revenge. He reminded his audience that we Americans all share important ideals. And he called on us to live up to our own high standards. Even though he did not single-handedly stop the retaliatory attack on Afghanistan that came later, he set a course that many peace movement leaders have followed ever since—steer by invoking the best American values. Peter was able to do what he did in 2001 because he had gained a good grasp of historic American values and metaphors.

The "One Big Family" Frame

By 2005 the situation in our country had changed dramatically. The short-lived national unity 9/11 had created was long gone. Bitter partisanship was becoming the rule, in defiance of an historic American metaphor I call the One Big Family Frame.[2] My first web essay on this topic was published by *Common Dreams* on February 2, 2005, circulated to The Metaphor Project Network, and subsequently cited in Wikipedia (without our knowledge or doing). The full text can be found in Chapter 5.

The One Big Family Frame has long been a vital part of the nation's Ideal American Identity Story. Our "one big national family" is like any real extended family—fractious but in the end functional. There are people in it who aren't like you, but they are still family. We all have to try to solve our problems together, despite our differences. Our Constitution and Bill of Rights are explicitly designed to keep our internal conflicts civil and balanced.

The story of the One Big Family Frame implies a historic American way of communal problem solving. Nationally, the operative description is "bipartisan," "pragmatic," "solution oriented," "common sense," "practical," "pulling together," and "working as a team." The most important thing about this One Big Family Frame is the way it evokes the feeling of being one big team working together. The team focuses on solving real problems, looking at what really works and what doesn't. It emphasizes what we agree on (saving public money, for example) and having a shared goal we work for, even if our reasons for wanting the same result differ. The process includes working out a rough consensus about shared goals, compromising here and there if the potential results are worth it, and tolerating our differences.

A key part of this One Big Family Frame that we all strongly support, at least in principle, is the core set of American public values: fairness, honesty, equal opportunity, democracy, freedom, and compassion. These values are drawn from both religious and secular ethics. The One Big Family Frame is still very much alive in today's political struggles, despite current partisan rancor. I believe we will see it begin to emerge again as our nation's socioeconomic crisis deepens. I have revisited this frame several times since 2005; my 2011 essay about it, "Use the One Big Family Frame!" is available on our website, in the American Politics section of the Examples pages.

From "Stay the Course" to "Course Change": The Whole Story

In November 2005 the late Representative John Murtha (PA), a well-known Democratic hawk, returned from a trip to Iraq, calling for a "bipartisan course change." But the term did not take off at the time. In June 2006, I began working with the National Declaration of Peace Campaign on language for their call to action. I urged them to feature a demand for a "change of course" or "a course change" in their call. My reason for picking up and foregrounding this classic American frame again was that it could serve as a deliberate mutation of the Bush administration's apparently unsinkable "stay the course" slogan.

Simultaneously, at the beginning of July 2006, I wrote a Metaphor Project web essay entitled "Talking about Iraq," which recommended the "course change" metaphor. (The full text is reprinted in Chapter 6.) The post was sent on July 7, 2006 to our national and international MP Network, which also includes local and national Democratic Party leaders. On July 13, I received an e-mail from Representative Murtha, calling for "course change" in Iraq, as part of an e-mail blast he sent to his own network of peace supporters and Democrats.[3] At this point, pundits, journalists, and politicians began referring to the need for a "course change" or a "change of course" or other variations of the phrase, in steadily increasing numbers. (This can be demonstrated by doing a Google search for the terms.)

By early November 2006, when President Bush was asked at a news conference if he still advocated "staying the course" in Iraq, he famously asserted he had never said that at all. By 2007, everyone—even the neocons and the Right—began using "course change." The phrase helped to provide political cover for General Petraeus's new Iraqi counterterrorism strategy: paying Iraqi chieftains and their men to help root out a newly arrived Al Qaeda in Iraq. At the time, this worked a lot better than shooting or bombing tribal leaders and their families.

Economic Justice and "Hard Work"

During the spring of 2005, The Metaphor Project was invited to cooperate with The SPIN Project on a publication about framing economic justice: *Words That Work: Messaging for Economic Justice*.[4] My essay, "Speaking American about Economic Justice," produced in collaboration with SPIN Project staff, was published in the booklet in June 2005. The essay was subsequently republished about a year later in greatly revised form on the website of The Opportunity Agenda, an organization devoted to fostering social justice and increased opportunity for all. The full text of "Talking Opportunity in America" can be found in chapter 8.

My suggestions in the essay were to talk about the way hard work deserves a fair reward, to use appropriate sports metaphors, and to picture government as an honest referee. We also included the importance of helping those who have been hindered by circumstances through no fault of their own.

As a follow-up to this publication, I continued working with then-Executive Director of the SPIN Project, Heath Wickline, on his

Telling American Stories presentation. Subsequently, in 2006, Wickline took his show all over the country. He demonstrated what telling American stories meant to groups of activists, non-profit communication directors, and funders. He was particularly well received by those working on immigration issues.

"Choose the Cool It Option!"

In the spring of 2007, many people feared that the Bush administration was preparing to attack Iran. In March, I was invited to address The Emergency Summit to Prevent War with Iran at U.C. Berkeley on ways to frame the issue. Representatives from 38 activist groups were present at the conference, including people from 10 local Democratic Clubs.

The language I suggested at that time was "cool it," or "choose the cool it option," as opposed to the nuclear option that U.S. leaders "would not take off the table." A participant later told me that the only time people in the audience were taking notes was during my presentation. My suggestions were also sent as the March 2007 Metaphor Project post to our network, with the title "Re Iran: The 'Cool It' Option." The language was widely used by antiwar activists all over the country in campaigning against an attack on Iran.

I continued to work with a framing subcommittee on this issue until we had a poster with a good graphic, using the suggested language. My June 2007 Metaphor Project post, "The Iran Trap," carried on this work and received immediate praise from well-known progressive leaders David Korten and David Hartsough. The latter forwarded the message to his entire Iran antiwar network. One participant later heard Senator Diane Feinstein (D-CA) publicly advising the Bush administration to "cool the rhetoric." Subsequently, the "cool it" frame was also adopted by anti-global warming activists. Both of these essays are available in the Examples archive on our website, and the "Cool It" essay is reprinted in Chapter 6.

"The Grassroots Stimulus Story"

"The Grassroots Stimulus Story," our March 2009 MP essay, was also very well received. It suggested that citizen self-help efforts to create new barter networks, urban gardening cooperatives, and other kinds of close-to-the-ground, do-it-yourself economic recovery tools should receive more media attention and support. In the essay I went on to point out that we need a strong grassroots movement to deal with the long-term social, economic, and ecological crises moving toward us, to say nothing of the recession we currently face. The full text can be found in Chapter 8.

This web essay was immediately reprinted in a blog written by Grace Lee Boggs, an internationally known community organizer and trainer based in Detroit. It was also republished in *The Michigan Citizen*, a progressive weekly that serves the greater Detroit area. Subsequent to publication, coincidentally or not, coverage of grassroots efforts of the type I described did perceptibly increase for a while, appearing in *TIME* and *The New York Times*.

"Say Rules, not Regulation!"

Another example of "framing it American" success comes from our January 2010 post, "Say 'Rules,' not 'Regulation,'" found in Chapter 8. It was enthusiastically tweeted by David Korten as soon as it came out. Immediately after it was sent to our MP Network, and published in my diary on the *Daily Kos*, as well as on *OpEdNews*, the use of "rules" in place of the word "regulation" skyrocketed in political circles, along with some of the other sports metaphors I had recommended for talking about banking reform. A nice variation also occurred—I heard that one member of Congress suggested an excellent traffic metaphor variation: "Follow the rules of the road or get killed!"

The examples of American Framing given above are described more fully in the selection of Metaphor Project articles that follow. Publishing web essays on specific American frames for current political issues continues to be one of the most important functions of The Metaphor Project. Many of the American frames described in these articles have played a role, in one form or another, in some of the most important political debates of our times. Framing It American works! All of the American Framing suggestions found in these web essays were created using the process and tools described in Part III: How to Frame It American. Read through the essays in this section to get a clearer idea of how American Framing works. Then get down to doing it yourself in Part III!

CHAPTER 5

On Framing American Politics

The essays in this chapter have been included because they still carry much-needed lessons for progressives about American Framing as a key to American political persuasion.

⋖⋘⋙⋗

Countering the Right's "American" Con

(This piece was originally published on *OpEdNews,* on the *Daily Kos,* and was sent to The Metaphor Project Network on November 18, 2010. A revised version of it was published in the *Quaker Eco-Bulletin,* January-February 2011 issue.)

Although those on the Right claim their recent win justifies downsizing government, everyone now knows they just plan to stop Obama. Anything else they said is just a big con. But it's an "American" con. We progressives need to understand this much better over the next two years.

Very often, when the public votes the way they did on November 2, we shake our heads about the way they "vote against their interests." The explanations we give for it usually include the following: 1) People don't have the facts because of Fox, or talk radio, or the captive media; 2) The Democrats talk about policies and programs, not moral values; 3) People vote for those they identify with most closely, not the Democrats; 4) President Obama refuses to fight openly for a progressive agenda, or to demand more than he thinks he can get, even as smart public relations. Then there's the current favorite for number 5: The Democrats don't have a winning "narrative."

Make that "The Democrats didn't have a winning American story," and you'll get a lot closer to the whole truth. The subset of voters who turned out for the midterm elections identified with those who had an American story that matched the times, their feelings, and their beliefs.[1] So let's look more closely at what that story was.

The Right highlighted two elements of The Ideal American Identity Story this time. The first is the idea of *freedom*—freedom from any constraints on the action of individuals. This rebellion against any community rules, pressure, or constraint is a founding piece of the American character. Americans can be very easily scared by the idea that someone is going to take away their freedom. And they continue to believe that individual freedom is the key to American prosperity.

The second American story idea the Right used is a little more complex: essentially, it's about *being responsible*. In this case it involved fear of being controlled by a government that goes into deficit the way people as responsible individuals don't dare do, especially now.

To regain the lead, we progressives and Mr. Obama must find ways to tell a different American story about freedom, the deficit, and government. So what would a different American story about these things look like?

First of all, we need to raise our own red flags about freedom. Cut taxes for the super-rich and then cut Social Security and aid to the states to pay for it? Who is free if that happens? Who is truly free when there aren't enough government rules or cops to protect us from high-end, white collar crooks stealing from the people and getting off scot-free? So we could say: "Real freedom in America right now means freedom from being ripped off by the super-rich."

As for the idea that business should be "free" (again, no rules) to do all of the job-creating, and that tax cuts for the super-rich will somehow magically create those jobs, that's a free lunch for the super-rich, at taxpayer expense. Mountains of evidence show that only rising consumer demand creates jobs, not tax cuts for the super-rich or corporate CEOs. Give the rich the money, and they are free to pour it into the sea, for all we know or can trace. (A few media events featuring people dressed as top-hatted bigwigs pouring currency-green water into the ocean would be nice right now.)

Government-monitored tax credits, incentives, or programs are more accountable and responsible ways to give the economy a leg up. We can follow that money, because it leaves tracks. Even if by the time you read this, we've lost the fight to stop the next round of tax cuts for the super-rich, we need to keep repeating this message. Let's demand *responsible* accounting for the way the super-rich actually spend their tax cut money. That would be a nice public education follow-up, if it comes out that way.

Now let's look at the other big con the voting public seemed to buy: the idea that we should bring our federal deficit down right now by shrinking federal employment. But laid-off government employees would suddenly have no more money to spend on consumer goods, and they would start losing their houses too. Cut federal jobs and America bleeds faster. When others refuse to hire, government must prime the pump itself. Keeping its own people employed is the first step. That's the *responsible* thing to do. Public deficits are temporary; more wage earners fix them.

Of course, the most fundamental problem with the deficit issue is the household finance analogy. Individual voters have a legitimate fear of personal deficits these days. But there's an American story here too. If, as an individual, you find your expenses exceed your income, you don't simply cut everything. You also look for other sources of income! You get busy and try new things, like the responsible "can-do" American you are.

In hard times, as bitter recent experience shows, government is the only reliable backer of the American future, via traceable tax incentives, tax credits, new R AND D programs, outright purchases, or direct employment. If the economy stalls, government is the only agent we have with the responsibility to seed American jobs here at home.

Over the next two years, we must push our selfish, irresponsible elite and our wobbly president a lot harder. That means we should be telling our own American stories everywhere: online, offline, in the press, in person, and in the streets.

Cards on the Table!

(This piece was originally published on *OpEdNews*, the *Daily Kos*, and was sent to The Metaphor Project Network on April 29, 2010.)

Right now, the biggest game on Capitol Hill is the financial reform bill. Although the outcome is still far from sure, the Democrats are finally getting their narrative on this topic right, moving into American "punch back fighter" mode. They're countering Republican and Chamber of Commerce propaganda immediately. They're "stepping up to the plate" and demanding that legislators and tycoons "do the right thing" by the American people.[2]

But if the Democrats succeed in passing a decent financial reform bill, or even a just-barely-good-enough bill, there is something else they'd better do next before moving on to the energy bill, the immigration bill, the new START treaty, or whatever else they've got on their list.

That something is a vital piece of their "punch back" reform story: the "DISCLOSE" bill, unveiled today by Senator Charles Schumer (D-NY)and Representative Chris Van Hollen (D-MD).[3] It's designed to counter the damage the Supreme Court did us all with its Citizens United decision to allow unlimited corporate money in electioneering. The DISCLOSE bill will require big corporate or union ad backers to declare that "yes, they approved this ad," and it should prevent them from hiding behind "dummy organizations and sham groups" with deceptive names.[4]

It's time we the people called their bluff and made big corporate thieves put their personal (business) cards on the table. That includes flushing out the "U.S." Chamber of Commerce. Top-flight investigative reporting has consistently shown that the Chamber's policies and actions are now dominated by a shrinking number of retro-corporations actively fighting our much-needed shift to a green energy economy.[5] Talk about betting wrong! That's pretty far from representing all of American business these days.

The DISCLOSE bill sounds like the real "punch back" thing, and it looks like a winner. Let's talk to everyone about making big corporate thugs "put their cards on the table!"

◄◄--►►

American "Truth Bites"

(This piece was originally sent to The Metaphor Project Network and published on the *Daily Kos* and The Metaphor Project website on September 10, 2008.)

Two words. Three. Sometimes four or five at the most. Smart, punchy ones that have rhythm. Phrases that grab attention, tell a quick story, sound kind of familiar.

Today, friends, that's what it's really going to take to save the world, our ecosphere here on planet earth, and our country. If it's ever going to be "morning in America," if we are ever truly going to become that "shining city on a hill," we progressives and our friends in politics had better learn how to create equally powerful American sound bites (like those two).

Unfortunately, today too many progressive pundits still give the impression that we must choose between sloppy, off-the-cuff sound bites and long, abstract talking points or policy statements. This is a major disservice to the progressive movement. The importance of well-framed sound bites as a first step in political communication cannot be overestimated. It's also well documented.

Even if you are a prominent national figure, when the political fight starts to get ugly, the only thing the public will really recall is a simple, viral American "truth bite." And you have to have those phrases ready all the time, not just on prime time or in TV ads full of information.

In the case of John McCain, for example, he's not just "Mr. McSame." He's also the "ex-maverick," now that he has sold his soul to the Bush program. Or a "fake copycat" who claims to be a change agent too ("change for the worse"). Or "just a 10% maverick," since he actually voted with the Bush Administration about 90% of the time in the last eight years. Moreover, he and his running mate tell "whoppers," not "lies." Words and phrases like these are not only catchy. They show a kind of folksy, popular wit the American public likes.

As former President Clinton has said, "we can litanize and analyze all we want, but until people can say it in a phrase, we're sunk."[6] Jonathan Alter remarks in "I'm Rubber, You're Glue," that "memorable lines, images, gaffes and monikers are like a piece of gum on the bottom of your shoe. They get your attention and may even shape your voting behavior. In the world of marketing, 'sticky branding' means intentionally creating an emotional attachment to a consumer product."[7]

Alter goes on to say that [in politics] it's vital to find "the quirky expression or colorful figure of speech that someone might actually remember." And he also points out that "The most common standard for stickiness is whether it fits into a pre-existing impression," giving as his example Bush's ill-fated remark about Homeland Security's management of the Katrina crisis: "Heck of a job, Brownie." Using pop culture references or other familiar, slightly altered phrases or names can ensure success. "Mr. McSame" is a good example of the latter.

But as Barbara O'Connor, Professor of Political Communication at Sacramento State University, observed after Obama's 2008 Saddleback Church interview was televised, "the [Democratic] party is very bad at labeling things that provide an umbrella for other positive memories. Democrats tend to mush around and don't give people slogans like 'morning in America,' which Reagan used to evoke a feeling of hope and promise in the country."[8] We progressives have some of the same problems.

So if we and our political friends want to "take back the American Dream" anytime soon, we'd better put our shoulders to the wheel right now and come up with some powerful, viral, American "truth bites." Reasonable remarks, long stories, or rants don't do the job nowadays.

To learn how to create American "truth bites," click on the American Framing Steps link on the home page at *www.metaphorproject.org*.

◄◄•►►

The Story That Works

(This is an edited 2010 version of a post originally sent to our list and published on the *Daily Kos* and our website on January 20, 2007.)

A great deal has been said of late about telling "new" progressive stories to counter current American assumptions about how things actually work. Some of the establishment stories are about ideas such as "the free market is fair," "discrimination is gone from America," "individuals can still make it today with no help from others," and "free trade helps everyone." I call this kind of American story the "instrumental type," to distinguish it from American stories that refer to our core American identity and values.

All too often, however, a "new" progressive story designed to counter an establishment story ends up being just a true story about how badly things are working right now, with a trailer of dry-as-dust policy ideas. This tactic doesn't work very well in the U.S.

Announcing a second wave of legislative goals for the new Congressional Democratic majority back in January 2007, Speaker of the House Nancy Pelosi characterized the new push (the Iraq war, the budget, immigration policy, and climate change) as the beginning of an "American Values" agenda. This tag evokes the most important story for us all—not a new one, but the ideal one, about our shared national dream, about how things should work in America: the best American story. It's the most powerful story for mainstream Americans. And it's not the same thing as contemporary assumptions about how things work now, here or abroad.

Even though our country fails again and again to live up to our best national values and repeatedly ignores the wisdom of American stories that demonstrate these values, anyone wishing to create real social change must frame his or her "new" story as a way to realize the dream embedded in the "best American story." It's the one we all know by heart. It matters not a bit that politicians like President Bush have misused the language of that story, papering over their lies with it.

We must give Americans the real thing.

-<--->-

Our One Big Family Frame

(This piece is a lightly edited 2011 version of the article that was originally published on *Common Dreams* on February 2, 2005.)

As the Bush Administration finishes setting forth its alarming vision for America, we must lay out our own "big vision" story. But a vital piece of that vision is the way we get to the future we want, starting from where we are now. Given the dangerous state of our republic and the need for strong bipartisan resistance to the Bush agenda, our vision must be framed to include everyone. That means it must be able to draw support from the increasingly unhappy moderate Republicans in Congress, and in our local communities, without compromising our own basic goals. So let's look more closely at how this could work.

Why the One Big Family Frame?

The phrase "unhappy moderate Republicans" refers, of course, to the current effects of Radical Right extremism on the Republican party. That extremism is fragmenting the conservative camp politically, so our focus now needs to be on their newly divergent views about policy issues, not on the ways their nuclear families work. Lumping all conservatives together at this point is downright suicidal.

We have to get beyond the "nuclear family" story. There is a historic American National Family metaphor, a little less pretty than the version Barack Obama described in his famous 2004 Democratic Convention speech. The historic American National Family Frame describes a country that operates like any real extended family: fractious but, for the most part, functional. There are people in it who aren't just like you, but they are still family, and we still have to try to solve our problems together, despite our differences.

In fact, the laws enshrined in the Constitution and the Bill of Rights are explicitly designed to try to keep these internal conflicts civil and balanced, and to stop self-destructive "war" models of domestic political life, literal or figurative. The story of this Extended Family Frame also implies a specific, historical American way of communal problem solving. Nationally, the operative descriptive words are "bipartisan," "pragmatic," "solution oriented," "common sense," "practical," "pulling together," "teamwork," "community building," and "finding common ground." Many of these terms also apply at the local level.

The most important thing about this One Big Family Frame is the way people focus on real problem solving together. They look at what really works and what doesn't, emphasize what they agree on (saving public money, for example), aim for a shared goal (even if their reasons for wanting the result differ), work out a rough consensus, and compromise here and there if the potential results are worth it. They tolerate each other's differences as part of the traditional American respect for variety, individuality, and difference of views.

In addition, this frame acknowledges that we all hold, at least in principle, the same set of basic American Public Moral Values: fairness, honesty, equal opportunity, democracy, freedom, and compassion. This truth allowed Bush to pull off his "Orwellian language" strategy. But now the chasm between the values he invoked and the results they cover up has gotten so big that even some in his own party are beginning to recoil.

What We Can Do with the One Big Family Frame

The easiest way to start using the One Big Family Frame in mainstream dialogue is to ask what problems in the nation or the community (or the world) people are worried about the most. I have heard George Lakoff say that if you ask, "What's wrong around here?" in a neighborhood, the operative metaphors will pop out in the answers. Asking that question in America leads immediately to the question of how to solve the problem. Keeping the context pragmatic, practical, results-oriented, realistic, inclusive of all stakeholders, and workable should help. "Working to build a better_____," being "community problem-solvers," "making a difference," "doing the right thing," and "getting something done," are all phrases that work to create the right tone.

But How Can the One Big Family Fit in Battlefield America?

To those who would object that this kind of framing for progressive ideas doesn't stand a chance in the current political climate of all-out partisan warfare by the Republican Right in Congress and in the media, I would suggest that we use the One Big Family itself to fight the Right's dangerous "war" model of American politics at home and abroad. Our frame can restore the true spirit of American community at home and then expand it to the world. This way our One Big Family story could grow to mean making sure that genuine freedom, real ownership capacity, true democracy, enduring social solidarity, and a toxin-free life are available to all the members of our human family, wherever they may live.

Although Republicans regularly take harsh disciplinary measures against rebels within their own ranks, we are already seeing striking new examples of patriotic political courage among moderate Congressional Republicans. I'm thinking of recent developments on nuclear issues and Social Security. We must build on these hopeful signs.

We must become the "new American common sense activists," "the new American problem-solvers," or "the new American pragmatists." We need to combine the best of that traditional American community spirit and value set with hot new ideas, wherever they come from in our country. It's who we really want to be anyway: Americans who represent the best of the past and of the future. So let's let into this club any others who also like the One Big Family story, regardless of how they were raised or their current party label.

CHAPTER 6

On Framing Peace

This chapter brings together pieces I wrote on "speaking American" about U.S. wars and threats of war going back to 2001. Sadly, these ideas about helpful language for countering the U.S. war machine continue to be all too necessary and applicable.

◄‹··›►

Framing Obama's Biggest AfPak Mistake

(This is a lightly edited version of a piece first published on the *Daily Kos* and sent to our MP Network on May 18, 2009.)

Last week resistant House members reported heavy presidential lobbying in favor of the war supplemental funding bill, which allocates only 10% of the money to diplomacy and development aid. This comes after the President has repeatedly said his administration would favor diplomacy and development over military options. It flies in the face of statements by a wide range of counterterrorism experts and high-ranking military personnel, including Petraeus, that there is no military solution to the problem of Afghanistan. Worst of all, the Administration made absolutely no effort to cut funding for drones and air strikes. President Obama owes the American people an apology and a course change.

If your goal is winning over a population and peeling them away from guerrillas in their midst, dropping bombs that kill mostly civilian grannies and grandpas, mommies, babies, and kids must be the stupidest public relations stunt ever conceived. Counterterrorism scholars agree that to succeed in counterinsurgency work, you have to *protect* the people.[1] It doesn't matter if the Taliban is using them as human shields. It also doesn't matter if we bag a few Taliban leaders that way every once in a while. As President Obama himself recently said about torture, the real issue is not about whether it works or not, it's about who we are and what it does to who we are. The same is true of the drone and air-strike attacks.

Our "death from the air" AfPak tactic is the ultimate morally corrupt outcome of the kind of tactic that Grant started in the American Civil War. He deliberately targeted civilians at Vicksburg. Even if we aren't deliberately gunning for civilians now, accepting that kind of "collateral damage," as the military calls it, is just plain wrong. As a patriotic American, I am sickened by the thought of our drone and air-strike bombing tactics. It's even worse than our having tortured people. Is this what America has come to—the land of the free, the brave, the noble Americans who stand for democracy and human rights?

Moreover, just as our torture tactics did, our air war tactics are turning the people abused by them against us and seeding new Taliban and Al Qaeda recruits in droves. Grant's "civilian targets" innovation took place in a world where there was no Internet or instant media exposure. Now we all truly live in McLuhan's global village. Everybody knows everything you are doing right away, especially if you're the biggest military power in the area.

According to a July 25th, 2008 Associated Press report, the Taliban have a very sophisticated communications strategy, just right for their audience. They and their sympathizers create "songs, religious chants, and poetry that appeal to Afghan nationalism and Islamic pride." These are available on audio cassettes, DVDs, and even as ring tones for cell phones, in addition to websites, pamphlets, magazines, and fliers.[2] This is the new "smart" war, and we are flunking.

Today Afghanistan (and now Pakistan too) form the latest horrible case study for the new reality in international politics—war simply doesn't work as counterterrorism strategy. Mr. President, change your AfPak course! Afghanistan is a snare set for the U.S. by Osama Bin Laden: a trap he has dug for us, a trick we are failing to see!

⋖⋖⋅⋅⊱⊱

Re Iran: The "Cool It" Option

(This piece was first sent to The Metaphor Project Network and published on our website on March 13, 2007.)

Most American progressives agree that a U.S. "preventive" strike on Iran, nuclear or not, would be stupid and self-destructive, as well as immoral and illegal under international law. Our challenge right now is to help foster broader public support for diplomacy, not war. So how should we talk to the media and mainstream public about it? Right now some national figures are rapidly herding too much of the country and Congress down the path to another, even more crazy war.

When the public is frightened and can't flee, they get ready to fight. So we need something quick and powerful to open a gap in that train of thought—a little emotional shock, a moment of slight emotional hesitation. Our first step has to be a powerful "surface frame" or sound bite—a "media wedge." A good media wedge makes people stop and wonder: "What's that?" "What does that mean?" It gives our talking points a chance to get heard. It also signals something about the direction our talking points will go. And in the case of a hot current issue, it has to have its own "internal hook" or link to the current debate.

So the "wedge" I am recommending on this issue right now is the "cool it" option. Or for the policy wonk crowd: the "cool and contain" option. These two media wedges are clearly hooked to the phrase "all options on the table" that politicians of all stripes are using right now in regard to Iran. That's the phrase Professor Lakoff has just deconstructed as being in fact nothing but a naked nuclear threat. Our "cool it" wedges are also familiar colloquial language and evoke other successful tension defusings, such as the peaceful end of the Cold War.

In the dialogue these sound bites can evoke, all the talking points that fit these frames can follow. For example, we might want to start with current signs of motion toward a positive outcome: we have just been sitting down with Iran and Syria about the Iraq issue. So "cooling it" is already a real potential. Another place we have just cooled it is North Korea. It's clear that carrots worked better than sticks in that situation, also.

Moreover, important experts and national figures have called for "cooling it." And the prestigious and bipartisan Iraq Study Group has strongly recommended direct negotiations with Iran over the other issues we have with them. (We might add here that most people do not know that the U.S. has been refusing to talk to Iran for about 28 years.) Iran has also just recently hosted a broadly representative delegation of American and British religious leaders. You can find a report on this visit and the religious leaders' recommendations on the highly respected website of the Friends Committee on National Legislation at: *www.fcnl.org.*

Responding to all of this widespread expert worry about what our reckless administration might do next about Iran, Senator Webb (D-VA) has also just introduced S759, expressly forbidding the administration to attack Iran without Congressional approval.

Next, in our talking points sequence, we could shift gears and talk about the Iranian people themselves. All of our worried experts—political and religious leaders—know that Iran is very different from Iraq:

A. It's much more of a democracy.

B. Many Iranian citizens are very unhappy with the current president, who does not have the ultimate power ours has, and that reality showed in their last election.

C. Iran has a pro-American middle class.

D. We'd be much better off encouraging those folks to oust their hothead president themselves.

So it would be self-destructive and crazy to "total" their country the way we did Iraq; we would have another failure on our hands. We can change course on Iran, too. Leading with the "cool it" option, or the "cool and contain" option invokes our national memory of other successful outcomes from diplomacy and restraint. Americans love success—let's remind them how to get it again.

Talking About Iraq

(This piece was first sent to our MP Network and published on our website on July 7, 2006.)

This post is in two parts: headlines with frames, followed by a rationale for the headlines. All of the suggestions below are designed for those who are trying to reach and move fence-sitting liberals and Democratic legislators, as well as the conflicted mainstream public (polls show the majority hate the war but are still unwilling to leave Iraq).

Part 1: Headlines

Start talking using the following:

- We need a "course correction" in Iraq.
- We need to "set a new course" in Iraq.
- We need to "change course" in Iraq.
- We need a "course change" in Iraq.

Then speak of the following:

- We have a new window of opportunity in Iraq right now.
- There is a lot of change in the Iraqi political situation now; we need to respond quickly to those changes.
- We need to listen to what the Iraqi government and other powerful Iraqi groups are saying now. They say they want the United States to help make a "handover plan." (Don't call it an "exit" plan; see below for why not.)

* We should seize the opportunity to give democracy a big boost in Iraq right now.

Talk about using the "handover plan" to:

* Help bring the American occupation (not "war") in Iraq to a better conclusion (don't use the phrase "to an end now"), because right now the Iraqis really don't trust us anymore to give their country or their oil back. Along with fighting each other, they are rebelling against us.

Part 2: Rationale

(This section includes further comments you could make about the recent bipartisan Congressional attempt to ban funding for permanent bases in Iraq).

The single most important disagreement we still have in the U.S. about the Iraq issue grows out of the notorious but very deep-seated "Pottery Barn analogy"—if you break it, you pay or you fix it. Many Americans who have come to hate this war are reluctant to join calls to simply "bring the troops home now," because they fear the civil war in Iraq will just get worse. They believe we would be responsible for leaving a failed state there, permanently reduced to medieval squalor. Moreover, that "now" plays right into the Republicans' "cut and run" definition of failure. As a people, Americans don't like failure. When the Republicans talk about "staying the course," "success," and "victory," it resonates deeply with them. Unfortunately, it keeps hope alive that we can still pull victory from the jaws of defeat in Iraq by using the same old bankrupt methods.

So if we progressives really want to win over mainstream opinion on Iraq and build a truly effective, multi-faceted push to conclude the failing occupation of Iraq, we are going to have to reframe our messages. We have to downplay that scary "drop that hot potato now/exit/end" failure frame. Phrases like "get out now/exit/end" all suggest a hasty rush out the fire exit, leaving the rest behind to burn—*The End*. Moreover, when we talk about "ending the war now," at this point the public thinks we are talking about the high-profile civil war in Iraq, and they don't believe our just walking out will stop that.

But we know that the only way to pull any kind of "success" from those genuinely looming failure jaws is to "set a new course," to make a big "course change," a major "course correction," because the situation on the ground in Iraq has really changed in big ways. These changes include more and more Iraqis themselves asking us to leave and proposing plans for how to do it. Moreover, reliable reporters say the Iraqis no longer trust us to leave and let them have their country and their oil back.

Iraqis say they think American forces are now playing favorites in the civil war, taking sides and being unfair. The fact that American soldiers have been guilty of torture and other atrocities is only making matters worse. This means that American forces aren't seen as peacekeepers by Iraqis now, because they are not seen as impartial. That's why we need an internationally led peacemaking process that includes warring Iraqi factions. Iraqis need real peacekeepers Iraqis can trust.

Moreover, an important change has already taken place right here in America. We have a new window of opportunity too. Both houses of Congress recently voted to ban funding for permanent bases. Although our administration leaned on the conference committee to strip out the ban, the Senate immediately passed it again. The original bipartisan vote against permanent bases is a huge step in the right direction. It sends a signal to the Iraqi people that there is a broad consensus in America about not staying forever in Iraq. We need to publicize this bipartisan vote everywhere, at home and abroad.

<--->

U.S. Moral Integrity Demands Crime Metaphor, Not War Metaphor

(This piece was sent to The MP Network and published on our website on September 14, 2001.)

The Letter to the Editor included below (already sent to *The San Francisco Chronicle*) represents the most concise and complete version of the message I believe we must get out to every member of Congress, every media outlet, and every opinion maker as quickly as possible. I have already contacted all of my own Congressional representatives with most of it (it has been evolving this morning).

Please use your own contact lists and forward this message as widely as possible, write versions of it to your own local newspapers, and do whatever else you can to create a buzz. The key part of it, I believe, is the issue of U.S. moral integrity. It is well-known that cognitive dissonance, the sense of being in conflict with oneself over value or meaning concepts, is one of the most powerful change agents there is. If George Lakoff is right about American politics (and I think he is), morality is the center of gravity in our political rhetoric.

Please do not fail to include the moral integrity point in your own versions of this message and the reference to McVeigh and "collateral damage," otherwise it will be too abstract.

If you would like to read an excellent and detailed argument for why calling the attack a "crime" is best, look at Michael Klare's piece entitled *How to Defeat bin Laden* at *www.salon.com*, dated September 13, 2001. Klare does not use the moral integrity/McVeigh references, but he includes brilliant ideas about how the "crime" definition can strengthen our ties to mainstream Islam worldwide and increase American understanding of the suffering of others abroad.

I feel very strongly that this terrible moment in our country's history offers us an unprecedented opportunity for growth and moral evolution. But this can only happen if we fully confront the moral gulf between responding to these bombings as "crime" or as "acts of war."

Dear Editor,

It is vital to our moral integrity as a nation that we immediately stop calling the bombings of New York and Washington acts of war. These attacks were crimes against humanity perpetrated by an international network of mass murderers. These crimes demand that justice be done. To react by calling for war brings us down to the same level as our attackers, because modern war involves the massive and systematic killing of innocents. The military's language for this, "collateral damage," is exactly how terrorist Timothy McVeigh dismissed the deaths of his innocent victims. Our country and our leaders must rise above this level now, before it is too late.

Your name

Your address

Your phone

CHAPTER 7

On Framing the Environment and Sustainability

The essays in this chapter contain suggestions for framing preventive action about the climate and sustainability crisis. They also point to some recurrent framing mistakes well-meaning American progressives make about these topics even today. To see sample results from a Metaphor Project workshop about environmental issues, take a look at Appendix II.

Framing Earthgate After Copenhagen

(This piece was published on *OpEdNews* on December 16, 2009. It is a revision of an earlier piece.)

Lately we've been hearing a lot about the need for more preventive healthcare, and rightly so. Private insurance companies have been unwilling to pay for it (what are they thinking?), and the uninsured can't afford it. We taxpayers end up covering the high cost of the emergency room result. However, the financial fallout from ignoring preventive healthcare will soon look like a pittance. Climate change-linked health problems are heading right for us, like a pod of rogue icebergs, with much worse to come — unless we act fast.

The price of delay in reducing CO_2 worldwide will be truly catastrophic, in healthcare costs alone. Our government, along with many others meeting in Copenhagen, is acting like the captain of the Titanic. The major corporations that control these governments have their heads in the sand. They are the same companies that control the U.S. Congress, which must produce climate change legislation soon. It's the biggest scandal ever: Earthgate.

People all over the world are stepping up their protests. Here at home we're going to need a much harder grassroots push too. And we'd better be "speaking American" about it. Let's start with the cost of treating climate change-related health problems. We can expect to see new tropical diseases invading areas where people have no resistance, new levels of respiratory illness, new heat stroke-related health disasters, and new epidemics. Though we may not be able to stop all of it at this point, we can certainly help prevent the worst — if our own Congress does the right thing.

But whatever we do to bring our government up to speed, we'd better be very savvy about the rest of our framing. As Hunter Lovins testifies in a recent documentary about environmental movement history, *Earth Days*, we lost 30 years of potential progress because of bad framing after the first Earth Day in 1970. As the film clearly shows, both the early environmental movement and President Carter said that the solution to our energy problems was to cut back, give up stuff, deny ourselves. This gave the Republicans and presidential hopeful Ronald Reagan a target. They used the underlying optimism and "can do" spirit embedded in the ideal American story against this negative narrative and they won. The solar panels Carter had put on the White House roof came down, and you know how this story ends — it's where we are today.

In the film, Stewart Brand says it well: To move Americans you have to appeal to their pride — to their belief that anything is possible. Reducing the climate change threat is possible, so let's do it, America! Let's do it in new and better ways. And doing it well will help our economy and our own wallets too. Congress, make sure you give us preventive earthcare too — it's the smartest healthcare there is!

◄◄--►►

An 11th Hour Sequel

(This piece was published on October 1, 2007 on *Common Dreams*.)

Leonardo DiCaprio's new film, *The 11th Hour*, is a valiant first crack at popularizing the facts about the whole "earth crisis." It's a good start on a very tough task, and it has a great interactive companion website, *www.the11thhouraction.com*, too. The film's hybrid genre, "disaster movie + expert testimony" makes sense for a first step. But it also set me thinking about sequels. What kind of follow-up film do we need to reach all the people in the malls and the corporate or congressional halls?

My first thought was that since we've had the "crisis" movie, the next one should be the "opportunity" film. Although some new possibilities were described in *The 11th Hour*, the main emphasis was on the wake-up call. But a lot of evidence already indicates that the public knows we're in deep trouble on this planet. Hope and belief that it's possible to stave off disaster are the things in shortest supply.

So my sequel idea might reach an even bigger mainstream audience. For the broadest possible appeal, we need a sequel that tells the story of a big dream come true: how America went green and saved the world. (This is the kind of storytelling Tom Atlee calls "Imagineering." See: *www.storyfieldconference.com/Imagineering.html* and *www.storyfieldconference.com/SFC-Atlee-Storycology.html*.) This sequel idea I'm dreaming of would use every modern cinematic trick in the digital bag to show how it would feel to actually live in such a world. Maybe the film should feature some characters who time-travel to that future world from a declining world like ours. The time travelers should have some mentors in the new world, the real *Second Life* we all are going to need. And this film should do some flashbacks, as the mentors tell exactly how the world got from the time travelers' sad reality to the mentors' hopeful one.

A lot of the narrative and visual details of this sequel—dying planet today, potentially green planet tomorrow—could be fleshed out from the testimony of the *The 11th Hour's* experts about solutions. The missing piece of my dream film script is the story of how we organized ourselves to get from our world to a better future. I would have Green world mentors tell our time travelers about the way consumer choice, citizen action, and corporate reform turned looming disaster into victory. Some nice flashbacks of this kind of action would help to make it real.

And the fact is that the "change story" *is* already starting to unfold! Right now we're seeing a cascade of new attention paid to the core of the "earth crisis" problem: the global corporatocracy's spiritual stranglehold on our efforts to save ourselves. Robert Reich's new book, *Supercapitalism*, is just the latest to lay out new details of how the supercapitalism vs. democracy bind works today. He suggests some powerful solutions. (For more on this topic, see Naomi Klein's newest, *The Shock Doctrine: The Rise of Disaster Capitalism*; Chalmers Johnson's latest, *Nemesis*; John Perkins' recent *Secret History of the American Empire*; and Peter Barnes' clearsighted *Capitalism 3.0*).

People aren't just reading about the supercapitalism problem either. The Fall 2007 issue of *YES! Magazine* is devoted to the wide range of organizing tactics and approaches people everywhere are using now. There's even a report in that issue about a very promising new joint effort, The Strategic Corporate Initiative.

The leaders of many of our own states are riding to the rescue too, way ahead of Washington in standing up to corporate foot dragging and political hamstringing on green issues. And, according to *The New York Times* (Sept. 16, 2007, "In Turnaround, Industries Seek U.S. Regulation"), some American industries are even beginning to beg for regulation now, so they can prepare better for the future of their businesses.

It all sounds like good film script material to me! And it's an American "can do" story, too.

-<-<--->->-

Framing Sustainability for the American Mainstream

(This is a memo prepared for the Marketing Action Subcommittee of the U.S. Partnership for the U.N. Decade of Education for Sustainability, November 2005.)

For successful framing, we have to understand what motivates mainstream Americans. In general, economic success or opportunity is the most powerful motivator to get the public moving toward sustainability, although it is best not to use the word "sustainability" for mainstream communication yet. We must frame it as being the key to our future economic success, and refer to the historical fact that technological innovation has been our most powerful creator of economic prosperity.

Americans also react strongly to threats—especially the economic threat of being left out (but take care not to use the phrase "left behind," as today it refers to the Religious Right's ideas about the coming Day of Judgment). We need to tap today's pervasive economic uneasiness, combined with traditional American optimism, love of all things new, and willingness to reinvent ourselves. If it fits the specific audience we have chosen, we might add moral or religious ideas of "creation care" or the spiritual calling to "earthcare." It is possible that in some quarters, an "ecological security" frame might work, but the "E" words (ecology, environment) must be used with caution.

Here are some examples of catch phrase or sound bite raw material that embody the kind of American frames described above:

- ◈ Moving toward/building a bright/brighter future

- ◈ Creating a new and better future

- ◈ Our/The New 21st Century American Dream

- ◈ Renewing/reclaiming/revitalizing the American Dream

- An America Reborn or An American Rebirth

- Keeping/Fulfilling The American Promise

- The American Promise Reborn

Another type of meta-frame not yet in sound bite form is the "Catch-up" model—America coming from behind, after being left out, suddenly really looking at what the rest of the world is doing. Some examples include the Sputnik shock and the original Apollo Program. Another is the way American automakers are now belatedly jumping on the hybrid bandwagon.

CHAPTER 8

On Framing Social and Economic Justice

This chapter covers some American Framing choices vital for promoting social and economic justice. To see examples from a Metaphor Project American Framing workshop on fair trade, take a look at Appendix II.

≺⊱⊰≻

Say "Rules," Not "Regulation"

(An earlier version of this piece was first published on January 17, 2010 on *OpEdNews* and the *Daily Kos*, and distributed to The MP Network.)

Right now, the ball is still up in the air on two issues vital to our future as a nation—financial system reform and energy policy reform. Some Congressional action has already occurred on each of these, but the games are not over yet. That's why it's so important that we get our metaphors right, as we move into the home stretch.

Maybe you've noticed the sports metaphors I'm using? These are the frames we should all be choosing now, for both issues. Most Americans pay close attention to sports and to sports metaphors. Sports metaphors are the most common kind in American political dialogue. And even though many progressives dislike sports metaphors for good reason, not all sports metaphors evoke the "winner takes all, competition is the only criterion" ideas we justly critique. The most useful sports metaphor for our purposes is "play by the rules," because it's the popular form of "follow the rule of law." That is a concept we can wholeheartedly support.

Moreover, every human activity, or "game," has rules, implicit or explicit. The biggest de facto lie of supply-side economics has been that markets or foreign trade can be "free." There's no such thing! Even a village market high in the Andes has unwritten rules of order and fairness, and trade agreements are nothing but a set of rules about how business will be conducted. Moreover, our planet's biosphere has iron rules. We are all going to pay very big penalties if we keep on breaking them.

Conservatives always scream about how "regulation" will harm business and our economy. In reality, that's just their way of demanding the right to play the economic game with no rules. Or to play the game with secret, arcane, or unstated rules that favor them cheating, stealing, being criminally negligent of public safety, and lying to the public about it. This is exactly why we need good government: We need an honest referee. (Yes, I know our government is compromised right now—publicly funded elections at every level should be the next really big "rules" fight.)

The first step right now is to talk about playing by the rules again, the rules that keep us safe and help us get fair and square, win-win outcomes for every American.

The Grassroots Stimulus Story

(An earlier version of this piece was first published on the *Daily Kos* on March 17, 2009, then republished by Grace Lee Boggs in her blog, and reprinted in *The Michigan Citizen* later that month.)

As the wheels of D.C. slowly crank out top-down recession solutions, out in the grassroots people are taking matters into their own hands. When Republicans decide to make life more miserable for the hardest-hit Americans, who dares rely on D.C. alone?

Some communities are getting more interested in urban gardening, local cooperatives, or trading and bartering events.[1] Others are banding together to assist those who have been foreclosed out of their homes.[2] Add to this the city and county greening projects already going on, far below the national radar, and you have a burgeoning unreported national trend.[3] And this list features just a few of the many possible bottom-up citizen initiatives.[4]

It's high time the media and our government took notice. This could be the biggest recovery story of all! Reporting what's happening now as a national trend will also help it gather speed. And speed is what we need. Although the President talks about using the economic crisis to jumpstart a green recovery, we'll need a lot more than top-down efforts to succeed.

Fostering bottom-up grassroots solutions is also sound science. Recovery from collapses, social, economic, or ecological, always starts close to the ground. Modern ecosystem research also shows that a bottom-up recovery can lead to a vastly improved system. Reporting in the latest *World Watch* magazine (March/April 2009), Thomas Homer-Dixon notes that collapse in nature "liberates... enormous potential for creativity and allows for novel and unpredictable recombination." The emerging pattern is "far less interconnected and rigid. . .and far more resilient to sudden shock." It encourages "new behaviors and relationships."[5]

History shows that human societies follow the same pattern. Our propensity to experiment and invent has always been the key to our survival. But we must actively foster that kind of reorganizing now—before a deeper collapse wipes out what we'll need to shape a new way of living.[6] We know there are much bigger crises ahead—the end of reasonably priced oil, major global warming ravages, and the onset of serious resource overshoot.[7] Maybe if we get going with a vigorous grassroots transformation now, we'll be able to ride out those storms too.

At this point though, the most important thing is the story: Collapse can lead to rebirth in a more resilient form. Including the grassroots piece of the story is vital. That bottom-up path calls on some of our best national traits too — our innovative, pragmatic, can-do, roll-up-your sleeves style, as we work together, close to home, helping to reinvent a new and healthier economy.

◄◄··►►

Talking Opportunity in America

(This piece was first published online in *The Opportunity Toolkit* by The Opportunity Agenda, in April 2006. An earlier version was published in June 2005 in *Words That Work*, a joint publication of The SPIN Project and the Tides Foundation.)

To create change, we must frame our messages as part of the hopeful American story — a story about what America should be. Fortunately, telling this story isn't much of a stretch, because it embodies our dream: a fair nation that consistently creates prosperity and protects opportunity for all. To best tell this story, we need to incorporate the words, images, and metaphors that evoke these ideal American values in our daily work. I call this method of framing "speaking American."

The Land of Opportunity

There is a persistent (if misguided) idea in our society that everyone already has the opportunity to succeed just by living in America. This idealized understanding of opportunity often combines in people's minds with the widely held belief in "individual responsibility." This is the idea that in America it is up to individuals to pull themselves up by their bootstraps. In this frame, those who fail just aren't trying hard enough.

On the face of it, this combination of ideas looks like a tough one for us to reframe. But right now there is a widespread feeling that the country is going in the wrong direction. Sad as it is, this situation is actually helpful for promoting expanded opportunity. Since more people are experiencing barriers to opportunity, more people are open to new ideas about how to expand opportunity. *Now* is the time to take control of the Opportunity Frame.

Play Fair: Sports Metaphors

Hard work is highly valued in America; it's the quickest and surest way to gain respect in this country. There is a strong sense that the American people's hard work has created our country's success. In the American story, hard work should also lead to individual success and advancement, so any conditions that block people from working as hard as they can are considered unfair. Anything that hampers people trying hard to better their lot is also viewed as unjust. The ideal American story dictates that everyone here should get a fair deal and an equal shot at success. The playing field needs to be level.

That means that we consider it unfair when people can't get ahead because of things like easily preventable illnesses, lack of basic education and skills, or even outright job discrimination based on race, ethnicity, or gender.

If all this talk about fair play, fair deals, fair shots, and level playing fields has you thinking about the NBA finals or the World Series, that's because Americans use a lot of sports metaphors to express deeply held ideas about what we value. In promoting the Opportunity Frame, effective metaphors include those that emphasize teamwork (in which all Americans are on the same team) and fair play for all, while avoiding the imagery of competition between Americans — or between different groups of Americans — for scarce resources. Also effective are metaphors that evoke tearing down the walls that block opportunity so that all Americans can work hard and contribute to the American team.

An American "Can Do" Attitude

Americans are optimists. They hate failure and love success. If the messages we choose to employ focus consistently on how our country is headed in the wrong direction, we risk alienating our audience.

The American story contains some clear norms about how to make a comeback. We "find out what works," and we "make it happen." We are the ones who can "change direction" and "move ahead on a new path." We know how to "remove blocks" and "improve conditions." And we "never give up." We develop smart, innovative, effective, participatory, empowering solutions. We "try harder," and we "build a better future for everyone."

Using enduring American images, phrases, ideas, and metaphors like these can make sure we evoke the best and most widely shared American values when we speak to mainstream audiences. "Speaking American" in this way can help you connect with people in a way they'll easily understand, reframe the debate about opportunity, and change minds.

PART III

How to Frame It American

Introduction to PART III

In Part I, you learned what American Framing is and why we need it. In Part II, you saw some examples of The Metaphor Project's own American Framing suggestions. Now it's time to get down to the nuts and bolts of learning how to do it yourself. After all is said and done, framing is an art as well as a science, and practice makes perfect.

First, relax! This process is actually fun. We recommend that you start by trying it with a small group of friends or colleagues. As I've said before, American Framing draws on much you already know about the American political lexicon. But you will be combining elements of it with your own message in a new way. That is the real secret of our American Framing Steps — more about that in Chapter 10. As you keep practicing, you'll gain the fluency in speaking American that I promised you.

Before you begin:

- ◈ Schedule your trial session for three hours of relaxed daylight time, when people are at their best.

- ◈ Have colored markers, masking tape, an easel and pad handy. (Two easels and pads are even better.)

- ◈ Choose a room that allows you to post about five pages of easel paper where everyone can see them.

To learn how to Frame It American, you will need to:

- ◆ Quickly read through both Chapter 9: American Framing Tools That Add Oomph! and Chapter 10: The American Framing Steps—Our Secret.

- ◆ Then follow the directions given in Chapter 10, taking as much time as you need to do each step well.

- ◆ As part of that process, you'll go back to the American Framing Tools in Chapter 9 a second time. The two lists included there, the American Story Elements, and the American Metaphor Categories, are some of our most important resources. You will be asked to select from each list some language that you think will help you express your message. (In Chapter 11, you'll find more lists of American Framing language. Those resources cover topics like "change," "breakthroughs," and which American story elements are preferred by political Reds, Blues, or Purples.)

- ◆ The next step in the American Framing process involves brainstorming to mix your "ingredients" together, so that they form some catchy, easy-to-understand phrases that carry your meaning.[1]

- ◆ In the last stage of the American Framing Steps, you'll stand back and coolly evaluate your results, using Chapter 10's Criteria for Successful Mainstream Framing. Then you'll pick out the best language you've created and tweak the rest until it improves. If you have the resources, you might get your results tested professionally. Or you can do your own informal polls to check the reception of your results.

- ◆ After you have learned how to do American Framing, we suggest that you form an ongoing group that meets regularly to do this work. After all, the opposition never sleeps! Why should we?

CHAPTER 9

American Framing Tools
That Add Oomph!

This chapter contains two of The Metaphor Project's most important American Framing tools: The American Story Elements List and The American Metaphor Categories List.[1] You already had a brief introduction to the American Story Elements List in Chapter 2. The American Metaphor Categories List also suggests language that can evoke pieces of our national story. It is organized in a different way — by specific framing categories, such as "nature" or "family." Using these two lists together allows you to come at the American Framing problem in a "binocular" way.

These two lists also include some themes or language that might at first seem uncomfortable to progressives. However, a skillful application of such elements can actually work in our favor. For example, in 2010, national legislators used the sports metaphor "play by the rules" to help strengthen public support for new financial regulations. Our language lists are designed to nudge you into recalling other useful language choices too.

The first time, read through the two lists that follow very quickly. Then go on to Chapter 10: The American Framing Steps. As part of that process, you'll return to the language lists in this chapter. At that point you'll pick out the language that seems most likely to help you move your message. Of course, if you spot likely possibilities during a first reading, it's okay to take note of them at that time. But be aware that your ideas might change as you work your way through the American Framing Steps.

Some American Story Elements that Evoke Core Values

The Metaphor Project's list of enduring American Story Elements contains a number of important themes found in The American

Cultural Story. That story combines our highest values, our idealized national character (think "identity"), and items drawn from
our actual historical experience.

- ❖ THE AMERICAN DREAM: pioneering; being on the frontier of something; creating the new, bright future; we
  invent ourselves because we are a "can do" people (or
  we reinvent, redeem, renew, rebuild, fix, or restore); we
  like things bigger, better, higher up, improved, fresh;
  we want more; we do what works; we solve problems;
  we're practical; we explore possibilities; we're optimistic; we win...

  (This category is also tightly linked to the next element,
  THE AMERICAN NATION. The more narrowly individual
  and materialist version of THE AMERICAN DREAM is
  covered in FREE TO SUCCEED below. For the common
  extension of THE AMERICAN DREAM into techfixes and
  cartoon magic, see MAN TO SUPERMAN below.)

- ❖ THE AMERICAN NATION: democratic self-government;
  a new kind of nation with a mission; beacon of hope;
  melting pot; cradle of freedom or liberty; democracy's
  defender, champion and missionary; home of equal opportunity, of hope, of choice, of fairness, and of people
  power; conscience of the world; rule of law; human
  rights; freedom of speech and religion; political rights;
  justice; respect; a classless society...

- ❖ FREE TO SUCCEED: there are no barriers; anyone can be
  Horatio Alger (individual economic potential); ambi-
  tion; self-reliance; entrepreneurship; hope for economic
  success; going from rags to riches; being good equals
  being rich; individual effort; innovate; compete; being a
  winner; win by hard work and being smart; make it big;
  do big things; striking it rich, showing grit, owning your

own home or business; having a good job and financial security; coming from behind, being on the map...

◆ We're on a Roll: hitting the road or the open road; taking the fast lane or being on the fast track; going; moving; moving forward, being on the move; being a mover and shaker; keeping things going; driving; rolling; accelerating; going toward something; no limits; moving at a fast pace; going online; taking a trip; traveling; making a journey; exploring; escaping; going into action...

◆ Small Town Security: clean; safe; secure; snug; belonging; familiar; traditional; stable; moral; loyal; respectful; friendly; doing things by consensus; being middle-of-the-road; balanced; compromising; cooperating; protecting; participating; honest; caring; orderly; showing common sense; saving; storing something up; being true or fair; practicing tough love; setting limits; home, sweet home; doing right; being just; having a heart; being innocent; being a community; a safety net; a network; being united; being tolerant...(An important variant of this element is the "Us vs. Them" story, which includes the supportive community of those fighting to make the American promise of fairness, equality, and opportunity come true for all Americans.)

◆ Man to Superman: the cowboy; the sheriff; American folk heroes like Paul Bunyan and John Henry; Clark Kent; Spiderman; Superwoman; Batman; Catwoman; Lara Croft; James Bond; MacGyver; Iron Man; scientific magic; super-seeds; super-genes; bionic people; the endless techfix; ...

◆ The American Nightmare: secrecy; deception; lies; conspiracy; stealth attacks; secret deals; threats to U.S.

sovereignty; violation of rights or rule of law; threats of any kind; going too far; soaking the taxpayers; breaking the budget; betraying the public trust; cheating the public; unfair business practices; fear of foreign attack or danger; discrimination; coercion; fear of landing on the street; pessimism; apathy; hopelessness; being victims; exploitation; spreading immorality; economic collapse; monsters, vampires, and hostile aliens or robots...

Some American Metaphor Categories

❖ SPORTS: play to win; play by the rules; play fair; fair play; the ball is still in play; be a team player; join the team; be a good sport; be a poor or sore loser; the best defense is a good offense; game of chance; call a bluff; level the playing field; target something; teaming up; win, lose, practice; be a heavy hitter; goal...(These metaphors are often applied to other topics, especially BUSINESS, POLITICS, or WAR.)

❖ BUSINESS: too big to fail; a business grows, one builds a business; watch the bottom line; triple bottom line; be profit- or customer-driven; add value; be lean and mean; get a competitive advantage; take out insurance; invest in_____; we owe you; you're in debt to us; that will cost you; overdrafts; you earned it; ____ is money in the bank; open the books; balance the books; cook the books; honest accounting; negligence; full disclosure; kickbacks; accountability; due diligence; contracts; income; deficit; the "suits"; tycoons; robber barons; poison pills...(Business metaphors are often applied to topics in POLITICS, SPORTS, WAR, and to personal life.)

❖ THE ECONOMY AND THE MARKET: is a casino; slows, speeds up, accelerates, grows, explodes, booms, shrinks, balloons, deflates, inflates, tanks, crashes; is healthy or sick; runs a deficit; runs a surplus; is fair or unfair; is a bubble about to burst; is a bull or a bear; people are consumers; economic activity is a game, a war, competitive; corporations are teams; employees are team members; money is the lifeblood of the economy; saving; spending; investing; deficit; debt; imbalance...(Metaphors from all other categories get applied here.)

◆ WAR: win the battle, lose the war; acceptable losses; acceptable risk; the war on _____; collateral damage; preemptive strike; the good fight, moral combat; warriors, our forces, our troops; war games; hold the fort; shock and awe; macho, tough, honor, glory; revenge; insurgents; counter-insurgency...(Some WAR metaphors move back out again to POLITICS, SPORTS, and BUSINESS topics.)

◆ SCIENCE, TECHNOLOGY, COMPUTERS, AND THE WEB: experiment, test; evolve, DNA; formula, be a tool; be a machine; have too many moving parts; have a screw loose; be a well-oiled machine; drive, roll, slide, chug; be a computer: online, offline, in default mode, to program, to be a program, up on the screen, download, upload, upgrade, tool up, go viral, remix, mashup, bug, crash, hardware, software, interface, data...(These terms are also used in POLITICS, SPORTS, WAR, BUSINESS, as well as personal life.)

◆ AMERICAN POLITICS AND POLITICAL CAMPAIGNS: all politics is local; retail politics; Joe Six Pack; keep it simple, stupid; it's the economy, stupid; Wall St. vs. Main St.; straw man; witch hunt; dance with the one that brung ya; big government; the people are citizens (not consumers); working families; special interests; third rail; pork; carrot and stick; poison pill amendments...(More metaphors may be transferred into this category than out of it. See also: AMERICAN HISTORY.)

◆ AMERICAN HISTORY: Don't Tread on Me (early American phrase); the Square Deal; the New Deal; the Fair Deal; the Real Deal (Truman); the Bad Deal; the Raw Deal (2011 Debt Crisis Bill), the New Frontier; the Great Society; the City on a Hill; Morning in America; the Bridge to the 21st Century…(These metaphors are usually applied in POLITICS.)

◆ WORK: work ethic; wages, pay; profit–sharing; get a raise; pay your dues; pay cuts; put in your time; full-time; sweat equity; join the union, brotherhood, coop-erative, labor; work hard, play hard; solidarity; the work week; the workplace; the assembly line; doing _____ for a living; benefits; having a job or career; career choice; overtime; overwork; the second shift; independent con-tractors; retraining; layoffs; unemployment; underem-ployment; unemployment benefits; furlough; jobless; jobless recovery; pension, retirement; leisure, vacation…

◆ HUMANS AND NATURE: America the beautiful (for natural beauty); nature is: a garden, a cornucopia, a re-source, a web of life, an organism (Gaia), our mother, our original home, God's creation, pure, cruel, wild, untamed, raw, red in tooth and claw, indifferent, bats last; nature is going into overshoot or breakdown; we need to be bioneers; earth is a marketplace or an econ-omy; to be a tree, river, mountain, lake, animal, plant, or vegetable; humans are hunters, taming the wild west or nature; we sow or plant the seeds of _____; some animals are man's best friend: the faithful dog, the trusty horse; cows: don't try to understand 'em, just rope and throw and brand 'em (from Rawhide); Lifeboat Earth; Spaceship Earth; carbon/ecological footprint;

ecological overdraft; Earth Overshoot Day; rotting, weeding, blooming, fertilizing, budding, harvesting, withering, plowing, evolving, growing...(Some terms such as these are used in POLITICS or BUSINESS. See HEALTH, THE BODY, AND FOOD for other nature/human metaphors.)

◆ CRIMINALS AND REBELS: drifter, outlaw, gangster; mastermind, henchmen, goon; robber, pirate, crook, thief, public enemy; cement booties; drive-bys; carjacks; gang rule; bait and switch; shell game, con; the law, law and order, cops, police work; justice; vice, gambling; characters such as Thelma and Louise, Butch Cassidy and the Sundance Kid, or The Grey Fox...(These terms are also used in WAR, POLITICS, and BUSINESS.)

◆ RELIGIOUS MODELS AND TERMS: to have faith; going on a wing and a prayer; to be in or get to heaven; having an afterlife; to practice good stewardship; to be a sin or to sin; to be evil; to go to hell; to forgive; to redeem; to renew; to be saved; revival; Armageddon; the Rapture...(Metaphors drawn from this category are used everywhere else in The American Cultural Narrative.)

◆ HUMANISM, SPIRITUALITY, AND SELF–IMPROVEMENT: to experience personal growth; to be connected; to embrace all being; to practice the power of positive thinking; to find inner peace...(Terms from this category may be applied to formal RELIGIOUS contexts too.)

◆ FAMILY AND PARTNERS: being or going home; hometown; heartland; cocooning; being born; the cradle; being a brother, sister, father, mother; husband, wife, partner, bride, groom; love affair; breaking up; dating, courting; wedding; divorce; having children, being pregnant, giving birth; being in the nursery; miscarriage; full-term…(Many from the Family category often get used with RELIGIOUS, POLITICAL, or TECH/SCIENCE topics.)

◆ HEALTH, THE BODY, AND FOOD: being healthy, healed, cured; being ill; dying; the grave; one foot in the grave; getting a leg up; being head and shoulders above; getting fit; no pain, no gain; what's cooking?; if it's too hot, get out of the kitchen; your goose is cooked; we're cooking now!; bread and butter; recipe, ingredients; chopping block; boiling or boiled; hard–boiled; raw; being fried… (These metaphors get transferred to almost all other topics. See also: SLANG.)

◆ LITERATURE: all the world's a stage; it was pure poetry; it's a fairy tale; it's a mystery; my life is an open book; acting a part, taking a role; it was melodrama, a tragedy, a comedy, epic. *As a source of quotes from plays, novels, biographies, poetry, or epics, applied in new ways:* "can't put new wine into old bottles," The Bible, *Matthew* 9:16; "dust thou art and to dust thou shalt return," *Genesis* 3:19; "birds of the same feather," Shakespeare, *Henry V*; "the green–eyed monster," Shakespeare, *Othello*; 'the green fuse,' Dylan Thomas, "The Force That Through the Green Fuse Drives the Flower"…

◆ ENTERTAINMENT: it's a dance, carnival, circus, soap opera, blockbuster, sequel, drama, dress rehearsal; to sing the same old song; to trumpet; to act out; to perform; to rehearse; to strike a familiar chord; to be a clown, boy toy, magician, puppet; be a riddle, puzzle; play hide and seek, musical chairs; *As a source of images or quotes from TV, movies, pop music, radio or the Web, applied in new ways*: "Go ahead… make my day," "We don't need no stinkin' badges," "May the Force be with you!,"

"Beam me up, Scotty," "Just the facts, ma'am," "Make him an offer he can't refuse"...

◆ GAMES, COMICS, CARTOONS, VIDEO AND COMPUTER GAMES: be like the Roadrunner, Dennis the Menace, Garfield, Mickey Mouse, Wile E. Coyote, Bugs Bunny, or any popular video and computer game or anime characters. This category also includes all other games, pastimes, or gaming characters or terms, including items such as Monopoly, puzzle, puzzle pieces, checkerboard, chessboard, checkmate, pawn etc., a bad or good hand, fold, shuffle, house of cards, poker face, domino effect...

◆ SLANG, POP CULTURE, CATCH PHRASES, AD SLOGANS, AND BRAND NAMES: don't go there; be cool, hot, retro, hip, awesome, 'bad'; there's no free lunch; he's on the wrong track; Got Milk?; SEX: wham, bam, thank you, Ma'am; put a bun in the oven; hookups; friends with benefits...

(For lists of American Framing language focused on "change" and "breakthroughs," or a comparison of which American story elements are preferred by political Reds, Blues, or Purples, see Chapter 11.)

CHAPTER 10

The American Framing Steps:
Our Secret

First, A Bit of a Road Map

Start by quickly reading through all 10 of the American Framing Steps that follow. Then go back and carefully make your way through the first five steps. After that, you'll return to Chapter 9 to use the two American Framing Tools included there. This time, you'll choose and record on easel sheets the most likely-looking language and metaphors from those lists, as well as others that occur to you then.

Our Secret

But right after you take note of your actual language choices, I recommend that you and your group take a short break. Get up, move around, have some tea or coffee or a little snack.

Why take a break here? A metaphor for what's going on in our American Framing Steps is bread making. First, we gather the ingredients, then we mix them, and after that we set the mixture aside for a short time and let it "rise." This break serves as vital preparation for the most important part of the process: the hour-long brainstorming session that follows.[1] Pausing is a proven way to strengthen spontaneous creativity. Under the right conditions, we humans can all brainstorm smart framing language, as shown in the examples I gave in Chapter 4: Some Mighty Metaphors and How They Happened.[2]

Brainstorming relies on *rapid cognition*: that's the label cognitive scientists apply now to what we used to call "intuition." At some point in any creative process, it's important to take your eye off the ball long enough to let your unconscious start to work, just the way yeast does. Although at first it might feel like you are just following hunches, cognitive psychologists who have studied rapid cognition find that it relies on "a kind of giant computer [in our minds] that quickly and quietly processes a lot of data."[3] Unconscious rapid cognition is also what most voters rely on when they decide how to vote.[4] They are "thinking" unconsciously, using the familiar conceptual and linguistic frames that express The American Cultural Narrative. They just aren't aware they're doing it.

The first seven steps of the American Framing process are designed to help you consciously prepare the elements of your message. We ask you to think deeply about your audience, your goals, and your language. The second part is the secret of The Metaphor Project's framing process. Via the timeout break and the brainstorm that follows, you get into the same state of rapid cognition most American voters use for their political decision-making. This shift makes your American Framing results much more powerful.

Since you have consciously prepared for it, you have a strategic advantage when you deliberately deploy your own rapid cognition. That combination helps you quickly find powerful language that can make your message move. Because you have gotten in sync with the voters' usual state of mind, you can do much better than you would by using scientific analysis or logic alone.

Trying to select specific framing language by thinking about a long list of policy details, talking points, or abstract values will not get you where you want to go either. The result of that mistake is usually lead-footed, out-of-touch verbiage no smart progressive should use. Political analysis tied to abstract language inevitably splits people off from the emotionally powerful, value-laden language of our shared American stories. Instead, you must get into the same cognitive state as the audience you hope to reach: the rapid cognition storytelling mode. Then you have a real chance of speaking the language your mainstream audience can hear.

Studying your audience and being willing to translate your message is vital preparation for American Framing. In fact, our 10 American Framing Steps are roughly the same as what most professional pollsters do to prepare their own polling questions. Their expensive, large-scale testing operations confirm or correct this preparatory work. Professional polling can be very useful to those who can afford it. But today, with political organizing moving online and going more and more grassroots, we all need to learn how to "frame it American."

American Framing in 10 Steps

STEP 1: Identify your audience

Be clear about who your specific audience is. Spell it out in detail on your easel pad.

STEP 2: Listen to your audience

Take note of how your audience currently talks about your issue. If possible, ask some representatives directly. Pay close attention to what phrases, images, or metaphors they use. Make a list of these. Warning: While conventional polling may give you answers about your audience's position, it won't necessarily record their images or metaphors.

STEP 3: Consider the views of your audience

Consider your audience's beliefs, assumptions and feelings. How do they react to your issue? Add these to your notes about your audience. Plan to acknowledge your audience's feelings in an empathic way at the beginning of your message. A great deal has been said in recent years about empathy being a progressive value. You can model empathy by giving your audience the feeling that you understand them.

STEP 4: Use everyday language

Use simple, everyday language to summarize your message. Avoid the following:

- long, abstract, multisyllabic words (like "mul-ti-syl-lab-ic")

- complex arguments and explanations

- professional or scientific jargon, insider language such as "corporate greed," and acronyms

- lots of reasons, facts, and statistics, especially at the beginning of your message

- historical analysis

- attacking America, Americans, or the flag, by name or implication

STEP 5: Present your message as a problem-solving story

Organize your own message as a story of potentially successful problem solving, using all of the tools included below. Read through this whole section before completing this step.

A. Use problem-solving story queries

Develop your own story using the queries listed below. Many framing teachers also advise developing a story that has clear heroes, victims, and villains.[5] While this is very good advice, even more important is recognizing that most Americans want answers to the following practical questions in their stories:

- What's the problem?

- What will work to solve it, in the current context?

- What should we do right now?

* What should we do next?

* Who is "we"?

B. Define your proposed solution

Right now is also the time to decide what kind of solution you are proposing: a better but tried-and-true conventional solution, a change or mutation of an existing policy, or a brand new problem-solving idea. The nature of your solution will have an influence on the kind of language you should choose. For example:

* MAINSTREAMING WITH CONVENTIONAL REFRAMING
An example of conventional reframing is this: to counter "tax relief," try "Real patriots pay their share." Use conventional reframing when you want to show that your message fits the best American values, norms, and ideals we all share, as in "bright new future, can-do, rule of law, honest referee," or "play by the rules."

* MAINSTREAMING WITH A CONVENTIONAL MUTATION
An example of this kind of reframing is the way "course change" or "change course" replaced the Republicans' phrase, "stay the course," in the summer and fall of 2006. We at The Metaphor Project deliberately set loose these mutated conventional frames on the Web again that summer, and by the fall of 2006, they had spread to every corner of the American political arena.

All these mutated frames required was a little tweaking of the existing mantra, "stay the course." (See the Introduction to Part II for the whole 2006 "course change" story.) Other examples of conventional mutation include the many variations of "Got milk?" Here are just a few: "Got poodles?" "Got kosher?" "Got clean air?" "Got blood?"

Use mutation framing when you want to change an existing policy to another conventional solution by monkeying with the opposition's own language.

• MAINSTREAMING WITH NOVEL FRAMING
An example of a novel frame is the frankenfood family of words reported in Chapter 4. As I noted there, it has now spread to include "frankenfish," "frankentrees," and a host of other variations, including "frankenstate," "frankenseeds," and the latest (in 2010), "frankenbugs."

Mainstream with novel framing when you want to show that your message is about something brand new and urgent. When first introduced, novel frames can act like "wedges" inserted into the pell-mell rush of modern communications. They stop the process and make people say, "What?" or "What's that?" This gives activists a better chance to get a few more words in about their issue. The history of "frankenfood" is a classic example of this effect.

Other examples include: "terminator seeds" (seeds genetically modified to produce infertile offspring), "river of grass" (used in a campaign to protect the Everglades), "buffalo commons (used in a campaign also reported in Chapter 4) or "Choose the cool it option!" (used in anti-Iran attack organizing in 2007, described in the Introduction to Part II).

c. Include references to seeing, hearing, and feeling

Be sure to include references to seeing, hearing, and feeling the problem and the solution. This will help you reach people of all learning styles. Remember that establishing effective rapport with your audience is your most fundamental goal.[6] Below is an example of storytelling that also includes using the seeing, hearing, and feeling words:

- WHAT'S THE PROBLEM? We can all *see* that the root problem with our most recent economic crisis has been the lack of proper rules and regulation.

- WHAT WILL WORK TO SOLVE IT? Congress needs to *hear* and obey the people's voice in terms of ensuring firm and honest enforcement by the federal government.

- WHAT SHOULD WE DO RIGHT NOW? We need to show Congress, Wall Street, and the Administration how we *feel* by our actions.

- WHAT SHOULD WE DO NEXT? We need to let Congress know we citizens and voters are still *watching* them.

- WHO IS "WE"? Every *concerned* American taxpayer and voter needs to speak up loudly.

D. Write down the opposition's version of the story

This is also a good point in the American Framing process to write down the opposition's version of the story. Be sure to include the language they use. Doing that will keep their story fresh in your mind as you work through the rest of the American Framing Steps. This technique will also give you a preliminary sense of how strong your story will sound against theirs. (Remember, your goal is reaching the persuadable part of the mainstream American audience, not the hardcore opposition to your views.)

STEP 6: Pick out American story language

The next step in speaking American is picking out the American story words, phrases, metaphors, and images appropriate for communicating your message. American story language is the most effective carrier of our core values in everyday political communication. For example, if you mention being "on the move" in your message, you connect to a big piece of the American ideal of progress. If you talk about "everyone being in the same boat," you evoke our dream of a mutually supportive community. If you refer to "playing by the rules," you call up images of sports as a game with fair rules, and by implication, you also invoke the idea of rule by law.

Details of this step:

- ❖ REVIEW THE LISTS. Review the American Story Elements List and the American Metaphor Categories List in Chapter 9.

- ❖ PICK OUT THE BEST. Pick out the words, phrases, images, and metaphors that best match your values, message, and audience.

- ❖ MAKE A LIST. Make a list of the choices with the most potential. Post it where you can all see it.

  (For more lists of American Framing language about "change" or "breakthroughs," or a comparison of which American story elements are preferred by political Reds, Blues, or Purples, see Chapter 11.)

‹‹‑ Take your break here! ‑››

STEP 7: Review your lists

Go back and quickly review all of your lists: your audience's ideas, feelings, language, the problem-solving story you created in Step 5, and your choice of American story language.

STEP 8: Start brainstorming to "remix" your message

Use the brainstorming method to find ways to express your message in short, snappy phrases. You can do this with integrity, because it's translating your most important message into compact, attention-getting form. Your results can include framing language for both the problems you target and the solutions you propose. Remember, today we need to start with something that looks like a sound bite, catch phrase or tagline. If it's good enough, people will want to hear more about your topic.

This step is the secret to success with American Framing. It's where the "remix" of your message and American political language happens. It's like the place where two rivers come together to form a much bigger, stronger one. (A famous American example: The Allegheny and Monongahela Rivers join to form the mighty Ohio at Pittsburgh, PA.) The "remix" point in our American Framing process is the place where thinking, feeling, and storytelling spontaneously fuse together.

Relax and let all the ingredients you have collected combine with each other, via your own rapid cognition. Have fun and don't take this step too seriously right now. Don't worry if the process gets off to a slow start. Allow everyone to warm up at their own speed. Tweak what you or others create, but don't critique anything in this step. This is serious play, and play will create the best results in the long run.

Here are a few examples of results from past Metaphor Project workshops: "the 'we' generation" (community), "keep Space open space" (against Space weaponization), "outfox Fox" (needs no explanation!), "war builds strong terrorists," "future theft," "unhappy meal," "real patriots pay it forward." (There are more examples of Metaphor Project workshop results in Appendix II.)

Details of this step:

◆ SELECT TWO FACILITATORS. Select two people as facilitators: one to write down suggestions on the easel pad, and another to call on people as they get ideas. As your group warms up, this process will get faster and faster.

- ❖ ALLOW ENOUGH TIME FOR BRAINSTORMING. Allow at least an hour for free brainstorming, using at least five sheets of standard easel pad paper to note suggestions. Post them where they all are visible at once.

- ❖ FOSTER FREEDOM OF EXPRESSION. Foster complete freedom of expression, no matter how bad the suggestions are at first. People have to get warmed up for this process to work. Don't critique at all during the free brainstorming period. And don't despair; the results will definitely get better.

- ❖ PLAY WITH PREVIOUS SUGGESTIONS. Encourage people to make new creations by tweaking or playing with other suggestions that have already been made. (Note: This is not the same thing as critique.)

STEP 9: Critique your framed language

When you have at least five easel pages of language suggestions, stop the process and make a formal change to critique mode. Check your newly framed language against the MP Criteria for Successful Mainstream Framing (below) and revise your results as needed.

Details of this step:

- ❖ REVIEW AND APPLY CRITERIA. As a group, review the Criteria listed below; then very quickly go over your sheets of suggestions, using the applause rating method. Pick out and mark the ones that seem to have the most appeal.

- ❖ TWEAK AND COMBINE. Allow more creative tweaking or combining at this stage too.

- ❖ IDENTIFY LANGUAGE THAT NEEDS WORK. Mark ones that need just a bit more work with "NW" (Needs Work).

- ❖ TRANSCRIBE YOUR RESULTS. Get someone to transcribe your best results (and the NW items) and circulate them to the group. Encourage further creative tweaking as people work with them.

MP Criteria for Successful Mainstream Framing

The Metaphor Project's eight main criteria are based on a variety of sources. Along with insights from cognitive science, communications studies, and contemporary rhetorical theory, we use some ideas and language drawn from the world of advertising. Advertisers were among the first to do serious scientific research on what actually persuades audiences. While they are still pushing the envelope on what works with the public, the language that advertisers use to talk about their own work has the kind of visceral clarity and power our language needs too. It's high time that we learned how to use the full range of tools available.

1. Which of your results have "legs," as the saying goes? What does your "gut" say about them? Do they have what it takes to "go viral"?

2. Are they concrete and specific? Do they use simple language?

3. Which ones are broadly accessible now? Are they credible?

4. Do they tell a story or draw a picture favorable to your cause? Are they self-explanatory? Do they make use of a comparison to something familiar to most people?

5. Do they appeal to people's emotions? Do they evoke the best American values?

6. Do they point to what causes the problem? Do they suggest a solution to the problem? Do the negative ones imply a potentially empowering positive solution? (Example: "Treaty trap" implies that one could also get out of it, go around it, warn people of it, spring it, or stay out of it.)

7. Are they just the right conventional phrase or metaphor for the moment, or surprising tweaks of the familiar, or fresh new combinations? If the latter, do they create a new category, the way "frankenfood" does?

8. Do they have rhythm? What is it? Say them aloud to check. If something is hard or awkward to say aloud, it will be hard for the mind to take in too. Does the rhythm sound like it matches your message? Rhythm is an absolutely vital feature today. If you doubt that rhythm matters, consider the amazing modern growth of rap and hip hop. Moreover, a lively and attractive rhythm has always been the mark of good English prose.

Now think twice:

❖ Do your results really pass the audience accessibility test?

❖ Do they have mainstream audience appeal right now?

❖ Who might they offend? Is it worth it?

STEP 10: External Validation and Ongoing Process:

❖ TEST YOUR CREATIONS. Test your creations in the field, either informally in conversation, online, via social networking, or even by cold calls you make yourself. If you have the funding for it, do the testing professionally.

❖ SCHEDULE UPDATES. Set up an ongoing mainstreaming group in your organization to continually refresh and update your framing.

❖ To see some tips for how to use your results in conversation, see Chapter 11.

❖ If you have the following concerns, see Appendix III: Hot Issues in Framing:

  ⬩ Framing in the context of organizing

  ⬩ Framing for quick results vs. long-term success

  ⬩ Framing about people vs. policy

  ⬩ Framing for your base vs. a mainstream audience

CHAPTER 11

More American Framing Tools

This chapter contains some additional American Framing resources that can enrich your work:

- Some American "Change" Language

- Some American "Breakthrough" Language

- Appealing to Political Reds, Blues, and Purples

- Some Tips for Using Your Creations during a Conversation

‹‹--›-›

Some American "Change" Language

(This set of language suggestions includes views from many perspectives.)

Positive Ideas of Change

- Good will triumph.

- Everything new is good.

- Everything is possible.

- Innovation is good. Being innovative is good.

- Things will improve.

- Improvements are good. Everything can be improved.

- We can improve ourselves. New, improved...

- Are you better off now than you were before?

- We are making progress.

- Progress is our most important product.

- We can fix it. We can turn it around.

- We can find a cure.

- We can succeed with hard work.

- We can be socially mobile.

- We can move toward more security and prosperity.

- Hard work and long hours will make things better.

- Change is good. Change grows from choice.

- Change is constant. Change comes in continuous steps.

- Change grows out of self-expression.

- Change means continuous improvement and growth.

- Individuals make good changes happen.

- Teams make good changes happen.

- Leaders make good changes happen.

- One's old boy or old girl network will create the change.

- Desirable change comes from the people, the grassroots.

- Desirable change comes from the private sector.

- Desirable change comes from a techfix.

- Desirable change comes from government leveling the playing field.

- Desirable change comes from government stimulus.

- Desirable change comes from government regulation.

- Desirable change comes from getting government out of the way.

- Democracy creates positive change, choice, self-expression.

- Capitalism creates positive change, choice, self-expression.

- An aroused public will demand change.

- If people get mad, there will be change.

- If there is a big enough crowd, team, mob, or swarm, there will be change.

- If we are united, strength in numbers will create change.

- If we have a debate or discussion about it, change will occur.

What to Do about Bad Things

- We will throw the rascals out.

- Anything bad will be reformed, renewed, revitalized, redeemed, restored, saved, or purified.

- Anything bad will be controlled or eliminated: people, dirt, homelessness, etc.

Negative Ideas of Change

- We like home sweet home just the way it is.

- Things are getting worse.

- The country is changing for the worse.

- Things are getting out of control.

- The crooks at the top are winning.

- The terrorists/slackers at the bottom are winning.

Some American "Breakthrough" Language

(These language suggestions range from sudden breakthroughs to gradual ones, in no particular order.)

- break through [verb form]

- sudden insight
- a spark
- sparking
- an electrical charge
- charged
- charged up
- catalytic
- lightning flash
- an electrical current
- a strong current
- upping the ante
- rising to the challenge
- turbocharged
- a new synergy
- a new synthesis
- a new level of leverage
- sudden shift
- paradigm shift
- polar shift
- dramatic shift
- powerful shift
- a catalytic shift
- going beyond

- an absolute change
- stroke of genius
- new sense of power and confidence
- ramp up
- ramping up
- hyper-
- a transformation
- transforming
- awakening
- metamorphosis
- growing trend
- a fast-growing trend
- a surprise
- surprising
- unanticipated
- ripple effect
- being swept up/into/toward
- leaping the chasm
- quantum leap
- bridging the gap
- crossing the bridge
- opening the door
- crossing the threshold

- pushing through
- leapfrog
- making the leap
- flying
- taking flight
- take off
- taking off
- tipping point
- stepping into a fast current
- moving into the fast lane
- going through the door
- finding the key
- unlocking
- opening up
- breaking out
- dawning
- rising
- giving birth to
- a rebirth of
- crossing the frontier
- starting
- changing course
- breaking new ground

- ◈ leading the way
- ◈ launching
- ◈ springing up
- ◈ starting fresh
- ◈ fresh start
- ◈ overcoming
- ◈ unleashing
- ◈ blooming
- ◈ unfolding
- ◈ go ahead
- ◈ headway
- ◈ step up
- ◈ boost
- ◈ cracking the code/barrier

Appealing to Political Reds, Blues, and Purples

The Ideal American Identity Story contains a variety of elements. Some are more favored by conservatives, others more by liberals and progressives. In general, almost everyone agrees in principle with most of the ideal American vision items about what kind of nation we are supposed to be: free, equal, honest, fair, democratic, and so on. (See the American Nation story element in Chapter 9.

Red state conservatives of all types tend to put more emphasis on the Free to Succeed story element. They think that the private in-dividual is responsible alone, and that too much government or regulation poses a problem.

Blue state liberals and progressives are more in sympathy with the Small Town Security story element. They see protecting the common good of America as the rightful business of government. They put their emphasis on fostering healthy public community.

Because of a long process of Congressional "safe seat" redistricting, the most important category in American politics right now is purples: "moderate" Republicans disturbed by Radical Right excesses. This group believes in fiscal prudence in government and caution in international adventures (especially war), but shares blue concerns about public community and the common good. Though more socially conservative than blues, members of the purple group (those whom Lakoff calls "biconceptual") may tend toward economic populism in their beliefs and voting habits.

This means that purples often favor both Free to Succeed and Small Town Security elements. For the greatest message success, we must select and recombine appropriate aspects of these story elements in ways that appeal to the purple group.

Some Tips for Using Your Creations during a Conversation

1. ASK YOUR AUDIENCE. Start by asking your audience how they see the issue now, or by introducing a question about a current topic that can lead to your subject: what do they think of a current book, movie, news item, and so on? Listen carefully before you start speaking yourself.

2. EXPLAIN YOUR POSITION. Explain your own position with the framed message elements you have created in advance.

3. TRY A LEADING QUESTION. If your conversation partner does not respond well, try a leading question that appears to be a tangent from the initial topic, but leads to new ground. For example: If the topic is preemptively attacking another country, ask, "How can we build greater international support for the United States?"

Conclusion

This book sums up what has turned out to be the most important work of my life. I began teaching American Framing via The Metaphor Project in my late fifties, and 14 years later, I am still at it. The urgency of building progressive capacity to speak American about our issues has grown steadily over those years. Now I am handing my American Framing legacy in book form to you, dear reader, in hopes that you will be able to carry on the work. Use it to help us win back and improve our democracy, our American dream, and our country. Like the teacher I still am, I'm going to review what we have just covered, to make sure it's all clear.

In the introduction to this book, I promised to show you how to do American Framing with integrity, fluency, and success. In Part I: American Framing Gets America's Ear, I outlined the rationale for American Framing and presented one of our key Metaphor Project resources for evoking The Ideal American Identity Story. That section also included answers to the most common objections to "speaking American," plus an account of how some American activists have created powerful new political metaphors. Part II: More American Frames That Stuck covered the story of some key Metaphor Project language suggestions and the web essays that made them go viral. Part III: How to Frame It American presented a detailed introduction and walk-through of The Metaphor Project's American Framing Steps, substantially revised and updated. There I also explained the hidden connections between some key findings of modern cognitive science and the practical success our Metaphor Project tools and resources make possible.

If you have suggestions, comments, or your own examples of success with American Framing, we at The Metaphor Project would
love to hear from you. Please use the Contact link on our website
at *www.metaphorproject.org* to get in touch.

Resources

Live links for all URLs listed here, plus additional resources, are available on our website at: *www.metaphorproject.org*

American Studies

Aguilar, Rose, *Red Highways*, PoliPoint Press, Sausalito, CA, 2008, 228 PP.

Alinsky, Saul, *Rules for Radicals*, Vintage, New York, 1971, 196 PP.

Atlee, Tom, *Reflections on Evolutionary Activism*, Evolutionary Action Press, Eugene, Oregon, 2009, 344 PP.

Bacevich, Andrew J., *The Limits of Power*, Henry Holt and Company, New York, 2008, 213 PP.

Bellah, Robert, "Prophetic Religion in Democratic Society," *Essays in Deepening the American Dream #10*, The Fetzer Institute, Spring 2006, 25 PP.

Bellah, Robert, et.al, *Habits of the Heart*, University of California Press, Berkeley, 1985, 355 PP.

Block, Fred, "Creating A Moral Economy," *The Nation*, March 20, 2006, online archive.

Brock, David, *Blinded by the Right*, Crown Publishers, New York, 2002, 336 PP.

Brooks, David, *Bobos in Paradise*, Simon & Schuster, New York, 2000, 284 PP.

Carter, Jimmy, *Our Endangered Values: America's Moral Crisis*, Simon & Schuster, New York, 2005, 212 PP.

Church, Forrest, *The American Creed*, St. Martin's Press, New York, 2002, 168 PP.

DeToqueville, Alexis, *Democracy in America*, Mentor, New York, (1956 edition), 317 PP.

Feldman, Jeffrey, *Framing the Debate*, Ig Publishing, New York, 2007, 201 PP.

Fetzer Institute Series on *Deepening The American Dream*: This series includes many distinguished authors: *www.fetzer.org*

Fineman, Howard, *The Thirteen American Arguments*, Random House, New York, 2008, 306 PP.

Fischer, David Hackett, *Albion's Seed: Four British Folkways in America*, Oxford, New York, 1989, 946 PP.

Frank, Thomas, *What's the Matter with Kansas?*, Metropolitan Books, New York, 2004, 306 PP.

Franke-Ruta, Garance, "Remapping the Culture Debate," *The American Prospect*, February 2006, PP. 38–48.

Fulghum, Robert, *All I Really Need to Know I Learned in Kindergarten*, Villard Books, New York, 1990, 146 PP.

Gerzon, Mark, *A House Divided*, Tarcher/Putnam, New York, 1996, 327 PP.

Haidt, Jonathan: Another valuable resource for thinking about communicating with mainstream Americans is the work of Professor Jonathan Haidt. See the following websites:
www.civilpolitics.org
www.yourmorals.org

Hertsgaard, Mark, *The Eagle's Shadow*, Picador, New York, 2002, 259 PP.

Hughes, Richard, *Myths Americans Live By*, University of Illinois Press, Urbana and Chicago, 2004, 203 PP.

Jacoby, Susan, *The Age of American Unreason*, Vintage, New York, 2009, 384 PP.

Klein, Naomi, *The Shock Doctrine*, Picador, New York, 2007, 699 PP.

Kusnet, David, *Speaking American*, Thunder's Mouth Press, New York, 1992, 240 PP.

Lappé, Frances Moore, *Getting A Grip*, Small Planet Media, Cambridge, MA, 2007, 186 PP.

Lardner, James, and Nathaniel Loewentheil, *Thinking Big*, Berrett-Koehler, San Francisco, 2009, 103 PP.

Liu, Eric, and Nick Hanauer, *The True Patriot*, Sasquatch Books, Seattle, 2007, 130 PP.

Lux, Michael, *The Progressive Revolution: How the Best in America Came to Be*, John Wiley & Sons, Inc., Hoboken, New Jersey, 2009, 242 PP.

Mathews, Anne, *Where The Buffalo Roam*, Grove, New York, 1992, 193 PP.

McAdams, Dan, "Redemption and American Politics," *The Chronicle of Higher Education*, December 3, 2004, online archive.

Needleman, Jacob, *The American Soul*, Tarcher, New York, 2002, 371 PP.

Nunberg,Geoffrey, *Going Nucular*, Public Affairs, New York, 2004, 298 PP.

Nunberg, Geoffrey, *Talking Right*, Public Affairs, New York, 2006, 288 PP.

Nunberg, Geoffrey, *The Way We Talk Now*, Houghton Mifflin, Boston, 2001, 243 PP.

O'Neill, Moira, "Can't I Just Invent My Own Metaphors?" *Changing the Public Conversation about Social Problems, Issue #37*, FrameWorks Institute, July 1, 2007, *www.frameworkinstiture.org*

Polyani, Livia, *Telling the American Story*, Ablex Publishers Group, Norwood, NJ, 1985, 158 PP.

Popper, Deborah E., and Frank J. Popper, "The Buffalo Commons, Using Regional Metaphor to Envision the Future," *Wild Earth*, Winter 1999–2000, PP. 30–37.

Ray, Paul, and Sherry Anderson, *The Cultural Creatives*, New Harmony Books, New York, 2000, 384 PP. See also their *New Political Compass* (2002) available at: *www.yesmagazine.org/pdf/ NewPoliticalCompassV73.pdf*

Reich, Robert, *Reason*, Vintage, New York, 2004, 247 PP.

Reich, Robert, *Tales of a New America*, Random House, New York, 1987, 290 PP.

Reich, Robert, "The Lost Art of Democratic Narrative," *The New Republic*, March 28, 2005, online archive.

Savan, Leslie, *Slam Dunks and No-Brainers*, Knopf, New York, 2005, 340 PP.

Schurmann, Franz, *American Soul*, Mercury House, San Francisco, 1995, 231 PP.

Smith, Huston and Kendra Smith, "The Almost Chosen People," *Essays in Deepening the American Dream #9*, The Fetzer Institute, Spring 2006, 25 PP.

Stout, Linda, *Bridging the Class Divide*, Beacon Press, Boston, 1996, 192 PP.

Wallis, Jim, *God's Politics*, HarperCollins, New York, 2005, 384 PP.

Whitman, Christine Todd, *It's My Party Too*, Penguin, New York, 2005, 247 PP.

Wickline, Heath, *Telling American Stories*, a blog found at *www.tellingamericanstories.com*

Wolfe, Alan, *One Nation After All*, Penguin, New York, 1998, 359 PP.

Zinn, Howard, *A Peoples' History of The United States*, HarperCollins, 1999 edition, New York, 702 PP.

On Bridging to Enduring American Values and Cultural Narratives

The general importance of framing our own messages by "bridging" them to "enduring American values" has been validated by numerous polls and research projects reported by the FrameWorks Institute, The Strategic Values Project, and American Environics.

Search these sites for "bridging" and "framing":

www.frameworksinstitute.org, especially for *FrameWorks Ezine* Issue 1: "Bridging," which also has very clear advice about using metaphors for bridging under the section called "Rule No. 4: Use Metaphors to Bridge." See also *FrameWorks Ezine* Issue 29: Topic: "Framing Lessons from the Social Movements Literature," and "Metaphors and Simplifying Models,"in Chapter III, Thinking Strategically about Framing, *Framing Public Issues.*

See also *www.thebreakthrough.org* and *www.AmericanEnvironics.com*

Susan Nall Bales of the FrameWorks Institute has also written very clearly about the vital role of enduring American cultural metaphor in framing. Her essay, "Reframing Community Messages through Myths and Metaphors," can be found at: *www. c3.ucla.edu/toolbox/terms-concepts/strategic-frame- analysis/ reframing-community-messages-through-myths-and-metaphors*

Franklin D. Gilliam, Jr.'s, "From the Self Making Person to Opportunity for All: Rethinking Our Thinking on Race," is an excellent 2006 resource that demonstrates the progressive bridging process used with traditional American values: *www.spa.ucla.edu/dean/Memo.pdf*

On American Cultural Models, Identities and Worldviews

Cultural Logic: *www.culturallogic.com*

◄◄··►►

Metaphor and Social Change

For a good basic introduction to the field of metaphor studies, with an emphasis on social change and politics, see the references below.

Metaphor and Framing

Duncombe, Stephen, *Dream: Re-Imagining Progressive Politics in an Age of Fantasy*, The New Press, New York, 2007, 230 PP.

Gilette, Kyle, *Modern Progressive Values*, Commonweal Institute, June 2008, 39 PP.

Hawken, Paul, *Blessed Unrest*, Viking, New York, 2007, 343 PP.

Horn, Bernie, *Framing the Future*, Berrett-Koehler, San Francisco, 2008, 175 PP.

Johnson, Mark, *Philosophical Perspectives on Metaphor*, University of Minnesota Press, Minneapolis, 1981, 361 PP.

Kovecses, Zoltan, *Metaphor: A Practical Introduction*, Oxford University Press, New York, 2002, 285 PP.

Lakoff, George, *Don't Think of an Elephant: Know Your Values and Frame the Debate*, Chelsea Green, White River Junction, VT, 2004, 144 PP.

Lakoff, George, *Moral Politics*, University of Chicago Press, 1996, 413 PP.

Lakoff, George, "The Body Politic," *Whole Earth Review*, Fall 1999, PP. 23–25.

Lakoff, George, *The Political Mind*, Viking, New York, 2008, 292 PP.

Lakoff, George, *Thinking Points: Communicating Our American Values and Vision*, Farrar, Straus and Giroux, New York, 2006, 176 PP.

Lakoff, George, *Whose Freedom? The Battle Over America's Most Important Idea*, Farrar, Strauss and Giroux, New York, 2006, 277 PP.

Lakoff, George, *Women, Fire, and Dangerous Things,* University of Chicago Press, 1987, 614 PP.

Lakoff, George, and Mark Johnson, *Metaphors We Live By*, University of Chicago Press, 1980, 242 PP.

Lakoff, George, and Mark Johnson, *Philosophy in the Flesh,* Basic Books, New York, 1999, 624 PP.

Miller, Anne, *Metaphorically Selling*, Chiron Associates, New York, 2004, 168 PP.

Richards, I.A., *The Philosophy of Rhetoric*, Oxford University Press, New York, 1936, 138 PP.

Sapolsky, Robert, "This is Your Brain on Metaphors," *The New York Times,* November 14, 2010, online archive.

Shenker-Osorio, Anat, "Numbers and Sense," Netroots Nation 2011 Conference, *www.netrootsnation.org/node/1868*

Westen, Drew, *The Political Brain*, Public Affairs, New York, 2007, 457 PP.

Whole Earth Review, "Metaphors and Morality," special section in the Fall 1999 issue.

Zaltman, Gerald, and Lindsay H. Zaltman, *Marketing Metaphoria,* Harvard Business Press, Boston, 2008, 219 PP.

Metaphor Brainstorming as a Change Technique

www.brainstorming.co.uk/tutorials/historyofbrainstorming.html

Search *en.wikipedia.org* for "brainstorming." See also Note 1, Introduction to Part III of this book for recent studies in business settings.

-<··>-

Framing and Cognitive Rhetoric

See also the many resources and URLs regarding framing in the *Metaphor and Social Change* section of this bibliography. There are now innumerable articles available online about the newly popular topic of framing. Many of these cite additional framing resources, trainings, or organizations. A good way to find them is to search Google for "political framing guides" or "issue framing." (Avoid the search term "framing" without any modifiers, as it will lead you to picture framing or carpentry.)

Another interesting new development in this area is the field of e-Rhetoric, which is the study of the art of persuasion as expressed in digital form, implemented through modern technologies. The field is expanding rapidly, and universities are now offering courses in it. Search online for "e-Rhetoric" for more information.

See also *www.co-intelligence.org/* for a vast trove of valuable information on nonpartisan framing and collective intelligence created or gathered by founder Tom Atlee.

Sources Not Listed Under Metaphor and Social Change

Brock, Bernard L., Mark E. Huglen, James D. Klumpp, and Sharon Howell, *Making Sense of Political Ideology*, Rowman & Littlefield, New York, 2005, 147 PP.

Burke, Kenneth, *A Grammar of Motives*, University of California Press, Berkeley, CA, 1969, 563 PP.

Burke, Kenneth, *A Rhetoric of Motives*, University of California Press, Berkeley, CA, 1969, 340 PP.

Burke, Kenneth, *Counterstatement*, University of California Press, Berkeley, CA, 1968, 225 PP.

Dunlap, Louise, *Undoing the Silence: Six Tools for Social Change Writing*, New Village Press, Oakland, CA, 2007, 229 PP.

Feldman, Jeffrey, *Framing the Debate*, Ig Publishing, Brooklyn, 2007, 201 PP.

Goffman, Erving, *Frame Analysis*, Northeastern University Press, Boston, 1971, 586 PP.

Hartmann, Thom, *Cracking The Code*, Berrett-Koehler, San Francisco, 2007, 227 PP.

Heath, Chip, and Dan Heath, *Made to Stick*, Random House, New York, 2007, 291 PP.

Heinrichs, Jay, *Thank You For Arguing*, Three Rivers Press, New York, 2007, 316 PP. See also his website at *www.figarospeech.com*

Iyengar, Shanto, "Speaking of Values: The Framing of American Politics," Article 7, *The Forum*, Volume 3, Issue 3, 2005, 9 PP.

Luntz, Dr. Frank, *Words That Work: It's Not What You Say, It's What People Hear*, Hyperion, New York, 2007, 324 PP.

Orwell, George, "Politics and the English Language," in *A Collection of Essays*, Mariner Books, 1970, 336 PP.

Perelman, Chaim, and Lucie Obrechts-Tyteca, *The New Rhetoric*, Presses Universitaires de France, Paris, 1958, 576 PP.

Reinsborough, Patrick, and Doyle Canning, *Re:Imagining Change*, PM Press, Oakland, CA, 2010, 142 PP.

Tannen, Deborah, *Framing in Discourse*, Oxford University Press, New York, 1993, 263 PP.

◄◄·►►

Language and Media Work

Bonk, Kathy, Henry Griggs, and Emily Tynes, *The Jossey-Bass Guide to Strategic Communications for Nonprofits*, Jossey-Bass, San Francisco, 1999, 192 PP.

Carville, James, and Paul Begala, *Buck Up, Suck Up, and Come Back When You Foul Up*, Simon and Schuster, 2001, 221 PP.

Derber, Charles, *Hidden Power*, Berrett-Koehler, San Francisco, 2005, 323 PP.

Gladwell, Malcolm, *Blink*, Little Brown, Boston, 2005, 277 PP.

Gladwell, Malcolm, *The Tipping Point*, Little Brown, Boston, 2000, 279 PP.

Goodman, Andy, *Storytelling as Best Practice*, Second Edition, Andy Goodman, Los Angeles, 2004, 28 PP., available as a PDF at: *www.agoodmanonline.com*

Hazen, Don, and Lakshmi Chaudry, *Start Making Sense*, AlterNet and Chelsea Green, White River Junction, VT, 2005, 232 PP.

Johnson, Dennis Loy, and Valerie Merians, *What We Do Now,* Melville House Publishing, Hoboken, NJ, 2004, 203 PP.

Manilow, Marianne, *Media How To Guidebook,* Media Alliance, 1999 or latest edition.

Moyer, Bill, with JoAnn McAllister, Mary Lou Finley, and Steven Soifer, *Doing Democracy,* New Society, 2000: (PP. 30–41; on language and organizing).

Noonan, Peggy, *On Speaking Well,* Harper, 1998, 224 PP.

Peavey, Fran, *Strategic Questioning,* Crabgrass, San Francisco, 2001, 74 PP.

Pinker, Steven, *The Language Instinct,* William Morrow, New York, 1994, 525 PP.

Plotnik, Adam, *Spunk & Bite,* Random House, New York, 2005, 263 PP.

Salzman, Jason, *Making the News,* Westview Press, Boulder, 2003, 304 PP.

Shipley, David, and Will Schwalbe, *SEND,* Knopf, New York, 2010, 288 PP.

Stout, Linda, *Bridging the Class Divide,* Beacon Press, Boston, 1996, 192 PP.

Wallack, Laurence, Kate Woodruff, Lori Dorfman, and Iris Diaz, *News for a Change: An Advocate's Guide to Working with the Media,* Sage Publications, London, 1999, 168 PP.

Zinsser, William, *On Writing Well,* Harper, New York, 2006 (30th Anniversary Edition), 336 PP.

Zuniga, Markos Moulitsas, *Taking on the System,* Celebra (Penguin), New York, 2008, 275 PP.

APPENDIX I: Frames, Framing, and Metaphor Today

Today, there is some confusion out there about what the words "to frame," "frames," "framing," and even "metaphor" mean. In the past, "to frame" or "to do framing" meant "to shape your message" in a broadly persuasive process. It included you as the message giver, your audience, the context, the content, and the language of your message. Most communications trainers still talk about framing as the way issues are deliberately packaged—the arguments, proofs, words, phrases, everyday metaphors, and visual cues you select to trigger predictable responses in your audience.

But lately cognitive scientists have begun using the words "frame," "framing," and even "metaphor" somewhat differently from the way most practical communications trainers do. Cognitive scientists study conceptual metaphor categories or formulas like "life is a journey," and they speak of the "journey frame." When they say we should be careful about our framing, they usually mean we should pick the right conceptual metaphor category for an issue. For example, progressives have recently been advised to describe the economy as if it were like a car, not like a human body.[1]

However, most cognitive scientists don't supply much in the way of everyday language to express the conceptual metaphors or stories they recommend. That isn't their job as scientists. The Metaphor Project's American Framing process, resources, and tools form a bridge between these two ways of talking about framing.[2] We offer the American Framing Steps, a communication message builder designed to work with our lists of American political metaphor categories and ideal American story elements. We also provide examples of specific language that can express those categories and stories, to help stimulate your own thinking about suitable everyday metaphors. In addition, as issues emerge, The Metaphor Project often publishes "just in time," ad hoc recommendations for framing language via web essay or tweet.

Creative everyday metaphor is the key to genuinely inspired political leadership. For example, back in the 1990s, former President Clinton urged us to build a "bridge to the 21st century." FDR pushed the "New Deal," and President Obama urged us to "reinvent America" in his 2011

State of the Union speech. Anti-GMO activists use novel metaphors like "frankenfood" (Frankenstein + food) and "terminator seeds" (the Terminator + seeds) to get attention and signal big trouble ahead in our food system. And in the summer of 2011, Van Jones launched the "Rebuild the American Dream" movement.

Helping you find lively language for your messages is the essence of what we do at The Metaphor Project. If you have the time and money to test your American Framing results professionally, by all means do so.

Appendix II: Some Metaphor Project Workshop Results

Metaphor Project Eco-Workshop Examples, 1997–2002

Here are some creations generated from standard American themes or stories, using The Metaphor Project's American Framing Steps:

1. balancing our ecological (or environmental) budget, getting rid of the ecological deficit or debt, relying on ecological deficit financing, calling for an ecological audit

2. moving from the "me generation" to the "we generation"

3. "pioneering a new green economy," "bioneering the new green economy"

4. making, gearing up for, or moving into the Green Shift (change to a green society, economy)

5. better green than gone

6. making the Earth-, Planet-, or future-friendly choice

7. organic in every pot

Here are some families of other new combinations that have been tried out by writers, organizations, and politicians:

1. "HEALTHY" GROUP: healthy wealth, healthy community, healthy city ("clean" is a subset, as is "livable" in livable communities or livable world)

2. "SMART" GROUP: smart growth, Earth-smart car

3. "REVOLUTION" GROUP: the next industrial revolution ("next" is a category of its own), the clean revolution (Bill Ford, Chair of Ford Motors), the biophilia revolution (David Orr), eco-revolution

4. "ECO" GROUP: eco-society, eco-economy, eco-revolution, eco-renaissance, eco-economics, eco-food (opposite of frankenfood), eco-safe economy, ecotecture (Skip Wentz), eco-moguls (*TIME*, October 18, 1999), eco-pioneers, eco-tourism, ecocide, eco-smart living, eco-city, eco-village,

global eco-village, eco-shift, eco-lifestyle, eco-audit, eco-enlightenment, Ecozoic era (Thomas Berry), ecopolis, ecodemocracy

5. "BIO" GROUP: bioeconomics, biomimicry, bioneers, biorealism, biorenaissance, biophilia, bionomics, bioregionalism

6. "GREEN" GROUP: "how green are you?" (from a Costco newsletter, summer 1999), the Green GDP (U.S. Commerce Department), "Viridian Manifesto" (a new hip version of green announced in the summer 1999 issue of *Whole Earth Review*), "the Green era" (Matthew Fox), a green economy (*YES! Magazine*), a Global Green Deal (Mark Hertsgaard)

7. "EVOLUTIONARY" GROUP: the evolutionary corporation (*YES! Magazine*, Fall 1999), the evolutionary car (Toyota hybrid)

8. "NATURAL" GROUP: The Natural Step (Karl Henrik Robert), natural capitalism (Paul Hawken)

Some Eco-Slogan Tweaks

Ecocentric, not egocentric

Nature rules

The rule of nature's law (play on rule of law)

Trees are us

Got air? or Got oxygen? or Got water?

Look out for #1 (with a picture of earth)

It's our crib (teen and African-American slang for home, also with a picture of Earth)

The earth is the bottom line

Earth: it's the real thing

Earthwise

Lean and green

Lean and clean

Bill of eco-democracy rights

The clean air generation

Stop before you shop

The ultimate green experience

Manifest harmony

Minimize your impact

Barefoot solar luxury

The cooperative cure

Dot.commongood

Green grandeur

Use it and reuse it

Reuse it or lose it

Déjà use

War on waste

Hate makes waste

Green dream

Jesus recycles

Don't just do it, think about it

Just recycle

Win one for the planet

Solar security

We're a solar family

Double-glaze your house, not the planet (or: not the sky?)

Only you can prevent climate change

Do people change the climate? People do

Oil ill

Ecological security

Super-eco

Accumulitis

Earth: the lean green living machine

See the U.S.A. the hybrid way

The electric Winnebago

Plug in, turn on, take a drive

Sports futility vehicle

I can't believe I polluted the whole thing (a sticker for SUVs)

Friends don't let friends drive an SUV

The *real* SUV — a sustainable urban vehicle

Save our children's children

It's _____ o'clock. Do you know where your children's future is?

Got safe food?

Got clean air?

Got clean water?

Got any topsoil left?

Got a future on this planet?

Save a planet, go to heaven

The planet you save could be your own

Friends don't let friends trash our planet

Friends don't let friends eat genetically modified food

A free-range chicken in every pot

Bigger is a bummer

Invest in your planet

Keeping earth safe for life

Making earth safe for life

Earth awareness: the new new frontier

Fiddling while our planet starts to burn

Fiddling while our planet slowly burns

The mother of all crashes: not just stocks, not just computers, earth systems

Forest.gone (a play on .com)

Earth, the real world-wide web of life

The dead planet blues

The climate threat

Climate shock

Climate crash

Climate decay

The weather threat

Planet poison

Planet poisoners

Poisoning the planet

The sick planet plan

A sick planet kills

A sick planet kills people

Shall we pass on a better world or just pass on?

Earth: systems crash or soft landing?

True abundance (versus affluenza or accumulitis)

Some Notable Eco-Quotes

"The warm war"
>—Arlie Hochschild, referring to climate change political problems
>(*The Atlantic*, February 2001)

"People exploit what they have merely concluded to be of value,
but they defend what they love."
>— Wendell Berry (*Whole Earth Review*, Fall 2000)

"We don't have an environmental problem; we have family rela-
tionship problems (with nature)."
>—George Work, ecologically sustainable rancher

"transpartisan"
>—Don Beck, co-author of *Spiral Dynamics*

"the Evernet"
> —David Denby in "The Speed of Light," (*The New Yorker*, November 27, 2000)

"PAX GAIA"
> —Thomas Berry, (*YES! Magazine*, Winter 2001)

"Power is communion."
> — Carolyn Raffensberger, (*YES! Magazine*, Winter 2001)

"corporate democracy"
> — J. K. Galbraith's commentary on how the 2000 election was decided, via Tom Atlee's listserv

"tend and befriend"
> — Dr. Shelley E. Taylor, (*The Tending Instinct*, 2002)

"the tipping point"
> — Malcolm Gladwell, (*The Tipping Point*, 2000)

"Don't listen to the hate channel."
> — Carolyn Casey, on not letting individual haters get to you

"speciescide"
> — Don MacQueen, quoted in Richard Heinberg's *Muse Letter* #107, December 2000

"Bill of Responsibilities"
> — William McDonough at Bioneers, 2000

"Declaration of Interdependence"
> — Bioneers, 2000

"the Circle of Life"
> — Julia Butterfly Hill

❮‹··›❯

Results of a Metaphor Project Workshop on Fair Trade, June 19, 2001

(This workshop was given to members of the anti-FTAA Coalition in San Francisco at Global Exchange, on June 19, 2001, at the urging of Juliette Beck.)

Fair Trade Frames

Fast Track railroads workers

There is no FREE trade

Free trade is never free

Free trade means free labor

Fast Track muzzles Congress

Fast Track = crime in the suites

Free trade: Wall Street's drug of choice. Stop the addiction

Fast Track is the wrong track

Derail Fast Track

Free trade is just another phrase for nothing left to lose

FTAA gonna get yo mama

Some "Afterthought" Tweaks

Keep America Free — Stop Fast Track (or stop FTAA, reverse NAFTA, shrink the WTO, curb the World Bank). Stop the corporate Free Lunch. Fast Track is un-American. UnAmerican treaty rules, unAmerican treaties, unAmerican rules, or unAmerican trade rules or loan rules.

Favored Tweaks that Need More Work

Corporate trade is the new slave trade

Why do immigrants cross to California?
It's not the cheese, it's the _____

Fast Track to powerlessness

More global corporations, more local struggle

Revitalization = colonialism in our inner cities

Appendix III: Hot Issues in Framing

Framing vs. organizing

Since George Lakoff's rise to popular prominence in 2004, articles periodically appear in the progressive press that critique the "framing fad" as inadequate for social change or political success. In this case, it doesn't matter whether the critics mean "framing" as cognitive science or as choosing everyday political language in order to persuade an audience. No serious "framing" expert of any kind believes that framing is a substitute for organizing or finding effective political candidates. Nor has any serious organizing or campaigning been effective without good framing of the issues at stake. For best results, effective issue framing must be fully integrated with movement or campaign building.

Framing for quick results or long-term success

Some cognitive framing theorists feel that for best results, a whole system of widely agreed-upon progressive conceptual frames or metaphor formulas must be worked out and publicized over a long period of time. Only then will we be able to persuade anyone by using ordinary metaphors. In the meantime, we must do what we can to come up with mainstream language that a broad cross-section of the liberal and progressive community can join in using. This is something like a big do-it-yourself experiment for the short term, hopefully backed up by field research and focus group testing as we go along.

Framing individual problems or issues vs. framing to promote broad public policy

Leaders of the progressive movement are especially concerned about fostering framing that will promote broad public policy changes, rather than addressing a patchwork of single issues or the problems of individuals. This distinction is also reflected in recommendations by UCLA's Center for Communications and Community. They make a valuable distinction between two types of framing in the mass media: *episodic* (a story about an incident happening to one or more individuals) and *thematic* (reporting that places public issues in the broader context of general conditions or outcomes). They urge us to employ thematic reporting at all times.

Another way to describe thematic reporting is that it shows that the misfortune of one or more individuals represents the exploitation of a whole group of people (tenants, workers, would-be voters, or at-risk youth, for example). It makes plain that their reactions are caused by unfair or unjust (or illegal) conditions, set in motion by the behavior of powerful others. This kind of new thematic framing is also a vital way to counter the all too pervasive American "blame the victim" frame (i.e., "the victim is the responsible party" formula), especially when it comes to news about poor or oppressed people.

Framing for progressives and their base vs. framing to reach mainstream Americans

Activists have many different goals and audiences in their organizing. At times you may wish to activate your own constituencies, or those parts of the larger public who may already be sympathetic to your cause. At other times, you may need to reach as much of the voting public as possible. Choosing the most effective everyday metaphors and noting the conceptual metaphor formulas they evoke for your intended audience can be vital to success. Notice the order in which I stated that process. To develop effective framing for specific audiences requires studying how they actually speak and think first.

ACKNOWLEDGMENTS

This book would not have been possible without help and support of every kind from a great many people. Many members of the national and international Metaphor Project Network have given us valuable feedback over the 11 years that various versions of our website have been online. Those most intimately involved in helping to make this book version of The Metaphor Project a reality include: Bridget Connelly, Christina Bertea, Lois Jones, Sandra Lewis, Ed Bernbaum, and Robin Standish. Raines Cohen, Betsy Morris, Roger Pritchard, and Ken Lebensold have also been important in helping the work go on. Ann Hancock has long been a steady source of encouragement.

From the earliest days of The Metaphor Project, Tom Atlee, Kenoli Oleari, and John Abbe have been great sources of assistance. Other vital forms of support have come from Silvia Swigert, Randy Garcez, Louise Todd Cope, the late Richard Johnson, Robert Goodrich, and the Henry Massie Family Charitable Trust.

Among those who early on recognized the importance of The Metaphor Project's work are Van Jones, David Korten, Frances Moore Lappé, Andres Edwards, Professor Michael Nagler, Daniel Hunter, Grace Lee Boggs, Kate Forrest, John Javna, David Brodwin, Holly Minch, Doug Cohen, Jakada Imani, Cara Pike, Lucy Sells, Ken Butigan, David Hartsough, Peter Barnes, Jonathan Rowe, Juliette Beck, and Carol Brouillet. Their feedback has also been an important part of The Metaphor Project's development.

Dalya Massachi, of Writing for Community Success, provided expert editorial assistance and guidance throughout the book production process. Asher Davison did final proofreading. Robert Mackinlay, of Robert Mackinlay Photography, donated his services for the author's photograph. Sharon Constant, of Visible Ink Design, did the book design. Sharon Constant and I created the cover design. Last, but not least, I have my partner, Richard Strong, to thank for his patience and invaluable feedback over the many years it has taken this book and The Metaphor Project itself to take their present form.

About The Metaphor Project

We at The Metaphor Project believe in a world that works for all. To get there, American progressives need to be able to speak to a wide range of Americans. The Metaphor Project provides training and guidance on American Framing or "speaking American," as the most effective way to express our messages for this purpose. Speaking American is a specific technique for presenting new liberal and progressive ideas at the "big idea" level, in a concrete, easily accessible form. It means using commonly understood words, phrases, images, or metaphors that evoke the finest American values—the ones we also share at the conceptual level.

The Metaphor Project has been building activist capacity to speak American since 1997. That was the year that founder Susan C. Strong decided to make her next project addressing the progressive communication gap. With the help of an active board of expert directors and some consultants for specialized tasks, she has been fully engaged in the work ever since. She created the first version of our resource-rich website in 2000, which was followed by redesigns in 2006 and 2009. Today, The Metaphor Project website is listed in many online resource rosters, including those at The Commonweal Institute, *In These Times* (under Message Shapers in their Link Directory), NP Action, The Story of Stuff, The Sightline Institute, and Progressive Spirit.

Over the years, many progressive activists and leaders have learned how to mainstream their messages using our American Framing resources in workshops, through presentations, or by means of the free resources on our website. Our method integrates and applies the best theoretical insights from a wide range of fields, including contemporary cognitive science, modern communications studies, the New Rhetoric, American studies, and American history.

Our first Metaphor Project monthly web essay about framing a current issue went out to a select list of key progressive leaders in 2000. Our member activists routinely forward them to their own networks. (Sign up to join on our website.) Today our active Metaphor Project Network is both national and international. MP posts about political language have been published on such sites as *OpEdNews, Daily Kos, Common Dreams, AlterNet,* and *AlterNet's Echo Chamber* blog. MP articles have been included online in *Rachel's Precaution Reporter,* the New Jersey State Department of Environmental Protection's regular online press release, and on The Opportunity Agenda's website. We're also on Twitter under "@SusanCStrong."

The Metaphor Project was one of six framing resources named in the 2006 handbook *Fifty Simple Things You Can Do to Fight the Right.* (Watch out for the typo in the MP URL listed in the 2006 edition though! Try *www.metaphorproject.org* instead.) Hundreds of progressive activists have also heard our message about American Framing via interviews on nationally streamed radio stations such as KPFA and other Pacifica stations, as well as KVMR and KWMR.

The Metaphor Project has been covered in other kinds of venues too. Among them are: *The Associated Press, The Sacramento Bee, Terrain, The Daily Beast,* and *Bay Area Businesswoman.* MP Letters to the Editor have appeared in *The Nation, YES! Magazine,* and *The Progressive Populist.* MP print articles have been published in *Words That Work: Messaging for Economic Justice* (published by The *SPIN* Project and The Tides Foundation), *The Quaker Eco-Bulletin, The Michigan Citizen, Connections,* and many other venues.

For a list of some of the most important organizations we've been involved with over the years, see the "Some Groups Served" page on our website. In addition to talks and workshops, we provide individualized or group coaching in person, by telephone, or by national conference call.

To see a few amusing stories about the way our "six degrees of connection" MP network operates, please check Note 1 for the Introduction to Part II.

About Susan C. Strong

Susan C. Strong, Ph.D., founded The Metaphor Project in 1997. Her goal was to help progressives learn how to mainstream their messages by framing them as part of The Ideal American Identity Story. She brings a broad range of academic and activist experience to her work with The Metaphor Project.

From 1972 to 1985 she taught communication about contemporary issues at The University of California, Berkeley's Rhetoric Department and also at the Communications Department of St. Mary's College (1982–1985). She holds a Ph.D. in Comparative Literature, and her dissertation explored political metaphor in 18th century European literature — the seedbed of our American dream. Since leaving the academic world, she has continued to do interdisciplinary research in the fields of American studies, American political rhetoric, communications, metaphor and social change, cognitive science, framing, and other topics relevant to the work of The Metaphor Project.

Beginning in 1986, she focused her day-to-day work on serving as a communication trainer, activist leader, nonprofit staff writer, and columnist about issues of peace, environment, and ecological sustainability. She is a former Senior Research Associate at the Center for Economic Conversion (Mountain View, CA) and a former Peace Action National Board member, representing California. She also served as National Peace Action Strategy Co-Chair and was a cofounder of the original Peace Action Peace Economy Campaign. She was a cofounder of The "Who's Counting?" Project, as well.

Her writing has been published on *OpEdNews, AlterNet, Common Dreams, Rachel's Precaution Reporter,* the New Jersey State Department of Environmental Protection's regular online press release, and The Opportunity Agenda's website. Her work has also appeared in *The Christian Science Monitor, The Boston Review, The San Francisco Chronicle, The Sacramento Bee,* and *The Quaker Eco-Bulletin* and has been nationally syndicated by Pacific News Service and The Progressive Media Project, among others. In addition, she blogs on the *Daily Kos,* where her screen name is Susan C Strong. You can find her on Twitter with the same screen name. On LinkedIn, she is Susan C. Strong.

Endnotes

Complete citations for books not cited here in full are found in the Resources section.

Introduction

1. Amy Goodman, "A Long Train Ride," *San Francisco Chronicle*, January 21, 2009, online archive.

2. To see more about the difference between framing and metaphor in everyday language and "frames" and "conceptual metaphor" in cognitive science research, please see Appendix I: Frames, Framing, and Metaphor Today.

3. George Lakoff, *The Political Mind*, p. 34, and Drew Westen, *The Political Brain*, p. 146.

Chapter 1: why american framing gets america's ear

1. I first noticed the term "persuadables" in Bernie Horn's book, *Framing the Future*, p. 47. (Berrett-Koehler, San Francisco, 2008, 175 pp.)

2. Long after I began using the term "speaking American" to describe what The Metaphor Project teaches, I discovered a book entitled *Speaking American* by David Kusnet, published as a campaign guide for Democrats running in the 1992 election campaign. (Thunder's Mouth Press, New York, 1992, 240 pp.) Kusnet's book confirmed everything I had been saying about using the American story to create mainstream-accessible phrases. More recently, I discovered a biography of Michael Harrington, subtitled "Speaking American," by Robert Gorman (*Michael Harrington: Speaking American*, Routledge, London, 1995, 288 pp., out of print). George Lakoff defended Obama's "patriotic language" in "The Obama Code," *The Huffington Post*, February 24, 2009.

3. See Chapter 10 for more examples of "Got milk?" variations. The "Got science?" sound bite was sent to activists as a subject line in Union of Concerned Scientists e-mails posted in August, 2010.

4. Thom Hartmann, *Cracking the Code*, pp. 21–27.

5. Naomi Wolf, *The End of America*, Chelsea Green, White River Junction, VT, 2007, P. 27.

6. Martin Luther King, Jr.,"*I Have a Dream*," delivered August 28, 1963, at the Lincoln Memorial, Washington, DC, from text preserved in online archive at: *www.americanrhetoric.com/speeches/mlkihaveadream.htm*

7. The term "undocumented workers" is found in the Talking Points section of the Opportunity Agenda's website, in a paper entitled *Moving Forward Together: The Role of Immigrants in Economic Recovery*. This paper is based on talking points developed by the National Immigration Forum, America's Voice, and the Immigration Policy Center. It can be found on the Opportunity Agenda's website at: *opportunityagenda.org/files/field_file/Immigrants%20and%20the%20 Economy%20-%20Talking%20Points%20-%20Feb%202009_0.pdf*

8. This change in framing to "human beings" was recommended by speakers at the 2010 U.S. Social Forum in Detroit. "Undocumented persons" is a term used by University of California, Berkeley Chancellor Birgineau, quoted in *The San Francisco Chronicle* on January 12, 2011.

9. *The True Patriot*, P. 9.

10. Berrett-Koehler, San Francisco, 2008, 175 PP.

11. Horn, *Framing the Future*, PP. 103, 113, 115.

12. ibid., P. 116 and P. 121.

13. PP. 108–109, Celebra (Penguin) New York, 2008, 275 PP.

14. Patrick Reinsborough and Doyle Canning, *Re:Imagining Change*.

15. Anat Shenker-Osorio, in "Numbers and Sense," Netroots Nation 2011 Conference, *www.netrootsnation.org/node/1868*

CHAPTER 2: AMERICAN STORIES YOU CAN USE

1. Farrar, Straus, and Giroux, New York, 2006, 277 PP.

2. ibid., PP. 135–144.

3. Random House, New York, 2008, 306 PP.

4. Decades of communication research have confirmed the importance of this practice, which is called "bridging." See the Resources section of this book under the "American Studies" heading for some key

articles about this subject: field work by the FrameWorks Institute, The Strategic Values Project, and American Environics validates this point.

5. Lakoff refers to the power of cultural narrative in his analysis of the appeal of Anna Nicole Smith in *The Political Mind*, PP. 28–42.

6. In his classic study, *One Nation After All*, famed Boston University sociologist Alan Wolfe noted that Americans are often inconsistent with themselves, but do not seem bothered by it. As for story elements or metaphors that are in conflict with the ecological, peace-building direction we must move in now, please see the discussion of this point in Chapter 3.

7. *Tales of a New America*, Random House, New York, 1987, 290 PP.; see also "The Lost Art of Democratic Narrative," *The New Republic*, March 28, 2005, search *ebookbrowse.com*

8. Legendary Texas oil and gas executive T. Boone Pickens' plan was swiftly discredited by critics as being purely self-interested and not of much real benefit to climate change reduction. However, he remains a classic American example of the "triumphant individual."

9. For more books or articles on the topic of "American Studies," see the list in the Resources section of this book. These works are among the most important sources for our own Metaphor Project framing resources.

10. Flowers is the Director of the Lyndon Baines Johnson Presidential Library and Museum. Her booklet is entitled *The American Dream and the Economic Myth*, Spring 2007, #12. Pearson is the Director of the James MacGregor Academy of Leadership and Professor of Leadership Studies in the School of Public Policy, University of Maryland College Park; her booklet is called *Maturing the American Dream*, Winter 2009, #15. I highly recommend this series; copies of the essays are available free of charge from The Fetzer Institute, *www.fetzer.org*

11. The American Metaphor Categories List is a part of Chapter 9.

12. For a list that sorts the themes by which side favors them, see Chapter 11.

13. These Metaphor Project lists have been developed and validated through ongoing interdisciplinary research and experimentation. See the "American Studies" section in the Resources part of this book.

14. See the "American Studies" section in the Resources part of this book.

15. Some of the most impressive recent scholarship on this point comes from Richard Hughes, *Myths Americans Live By*, Jacob Needleman, *The American Soul*, and Alan Wolfe, *One Nation After All*. See also the "American Studies" section in the Resources part of this book for links to the work of Susan Nall Bales and her colleagues at the FrameWorks Institute.

CHAPTER 3: MORE ANSWERS FOR CRITICS, REBELS, AND THE CONFUSED

1. Cognitive scientists George Lakoff and Drew Westen both show that stories work best in their recent books, *The Political Mind* and *The Political Brain*.

2. I say "appear" or "seems" here, because in *The Political Mind*, Lakoff argues that this is an illusion, even for progressives. See what he says about brain change and social change on pages 1–15 of his book.

3. Suspicion of emotion was increased by the rise of Positivism, first articulated and promulgated by Auguste Comte in the early 19th century. Positivism generally stands for the idea that truth can only be found through sensory experience and the scientific method. It has sometimes been considered "scientism"—an ideology itself.

4. George Lakoff, *The Political Mind*, PP. 13–14.

5. Thom Hartmann in *Cracking the Code* and Andy Goodman in *Storytelling as Best Practice* summarize the voluminous research that proves this point.

6. For more on "American Truth Bites," see the essay by that name in Part II.

7. Random House, New York, 2007, P. 16.

8. *Rules for Radicals*, Chapter 3. Alinsky goes on to say that the good organizer "can communicate only within the areas of experience of his audience." Therefore, "he [or she] learns the local legends, anecdotes, values, idioms. He listens to small talk. He refrains from rhetoric foreign to the local culture," PP. 69–70.

9. Quoted in an interview with Andy Goodman, *Free Range Thinking*, October 2008 newsletter, P. 2.

10. This quote comes from a book review by Nicholas Thompson, entitled "Era with No Name," in the Sunday, August 3, 2008 *New York Times Book Review*, P. 22. The book being reviewed was *America Between the Wars: From 11/9 to 9/11* by Derek Chollet and James Goldgeier. Apparently, no one was ever able to come up with a succinct or evocative title for that short era in our nation's history (1989 to 2001). In frustration about this, Clinton made the remark cited here.

11. *Newsweek*, September 1, 2008, P. 53.

12. Cited from an article written for *AlterNet* on July 14, 2008, "The Bad Frame," in the Media and Technology section of *AlterNet*: *www.alternet.org/media/91355*

13. The term "battle of the story" is actually a technical phrase used in the framing technique of SmartMeme: *www.smartmeme.org*

14. Susan Nall Bales of FrameWorks Institute has written very clearly about the vital role of enduring American cultural metaphor in framing. Her essay, *"Reframing Community Messages through Myths and Metaphors,"* can be found at: *www.c3.ucla.edu/toolbox/terms-concepts/ strategic-frame-analysis/ reframing-community-messages-through-myths-and-metaphors*

15. *www.democracyschool.com/* and *www.bluegreenalliance.org/home*

16. Two outstanding books that have addressed the problem of American exceptionalism when applied to how we manage our domestic affairs are *The Age of American Unreason,* by Susan Jacoby and *The Limits of Power: The End of American Exceptionalism*, by Andrew Bacevich, Jr. An excellent book that explains the origins of this part of The American Cultural Narrative is *Myths Americans Live By*, by Richard Hughes.

17. *The Limits of Power: The End of American Exceptionalism*, p. 174.

18. "The Voice of Unconventional Wisdom," *The New York Review of Books*, November 11, 2010, online archive.

19. *The Fall of the US Empire—and Then What?* TRANSCEND University Press, 2009, 270 PP. Available from: *www.transcend.org/tup/*

20. Madeleine Bunting, "Bono Talks of US Crusade," *The Guardian*, June 16, 2005, online archive.

21. Public Affairs, New York, 2006, 288 PP.

22. Since 2004 George Lakoff has often used the term "Machiavellian language" to denote phrases used by the Right to manipulate the public.

23. OneAmerica's website is *www.weareoneamerica.org/* and the Spring 2010 issue of *YES! Magazine* may be found at: *www.yesmagazine.org/issues/america-the-remix/table-of-contents.*

24. Proposition 23 aimed to set aside the recently passed Assembly Bill 32, which mandated new sustainable energy measures for businesses and other kinds of operations across the entire state of California.

Chapter 4: some mighty metaphors and how they happened

1. Robert Sapolsky, "This is Your Brain on Metaphors," *The New York Times,* November 14, 2010, online archive.

2. We at The Metaphor Project had been doing what we could since 1997 to suggest more effective language and framing methods. See Part II of this book for some examples of our work. Starting in 2004, George Lakoff also reached many with his basic critique of progressive framing flaws.

3. Leslie Swan, *Slam Dunks and No-Brainers,* Knopf, New York, 2005, p. 42.

4. The most relevant Geoffrey Nunberg book on this topic is *Talking Right.*

5. Cumming's article was based on her book, *Uncertain Peril,* Beacon Press, Boston, 2008, 240 pp.

6. Anne Mathews, *Where the Buffalo Roam,* pp. 22–37.

7. Madeline Ostrander reported this interview, pp. 26–29.

8. This account comes from an interview with Dr. Paloma Pavel.

9. The book was published by Volcano Press/Kazan Books, Volcano, CA, text copyright 1982 and text and art copyright 1993.

10. *Pay It Forward* is described both as a philosophy, the film itself, and also the title of a book by Catherine Ryan Hyde, published in 1999. Wikipedia traces the philosophy back to Benjamin Franklin, with the first widely known use of the coinage "pay it forward" by the science fiction author Robert Heinlein in his book *Between Planets,* published in 1951.

11. In "The New Radicals," April 24, 2000, by Walter Kirn and colleagues: Juliette's exact words were: "We have lots of Lilliputians all acting autonomously and at the same time connected."

12. See Drew Westen's *The Political Brain*, George Lakoff's *The Political Mind*, and Malcolm Gladwell's *Blink*. Gladwell uses the term "rapid cognition" to describe this phenomenon in his survey of the field.

PART II: MORE AMERICAN FRAMES THAT STUCK

1. For a complete list of groups or representatives of groups we have helped directly, and for more about our history in general, please see the list of Groups Served and The Metaphor Project News on our website at *www.metaphorproject.org*. Moreover, I have been told directly by progressive leaders such as Jakada Imani, Executive Director of The Ella Baker Center, and Cara Pike, then Communications Director at Earthjustice, that they or their staff have used our site in their work every day. Over the life of The Metaphor Project we have also repeatedly received written proof from MP Network members that they have passed our material on to their own lists and to key contacts, who have evidently continued passing it on.

As evidence of the latter, I'll share a few amusing anecdotes that show our "six degrees of connection" power at work. In 2008 I attended the Campaign for America's Take Back America Conference in Washington, D.C. While there I started to introduce myself and The Metaphor Project to Celinda Lake, the renowned Democratic pollster. Before I could even finish my spiel, she announced that she knew very well who I was and what The Metaphor Project did! Ms. Lake has never been a direct member of The MP Network list, and the only way she could have found out about us was by "word of web or mouth."

Another example: At an April 2010 University of California, Berkeley fundraiser for an extern program, I approached Robert Reich, who had been the featured speaker, and with whom I had had some correspondence the previous fall. Before I could do more than identify myself, he asked me if I knew Bob Pitofsky, the former chairman of the Federal Trade Commission. He said Pitofsky was the person who had first told him about The Metaphor Project. In fact, I do not know Mr. Pitofsky at all, nor has he ever been on The MP Network list. If a former chairman of the Federal Trade Commission told Robert Reich, former Secretary of Labor, about The Metaphor Project, you can be pretty sure word of us has been going around D.C. for a while.

2. For proof that the One Big Family Frame exists and is still relevant, please see the "American Studies" section in Resources.

3. Representative Murtha's subject line for this post was: "Tell Republicans to cut the 'traitor talk.'"

4. This publication was available, the last time I checked, as a PDF accessed via the Publications link, on the SPIN Project website at *www.spinproject.org.*

Chapter 5: on framing american politics

1. I'm aware that recent post-election polls suggest that many people who voted Republican were not actually voting for the specific measures politicians on the Right proposed. These findings actually strengthen my point that it was the Right's overall "American story" that made the difference.

2. This was Senator Schumer's language in a recent statement about the financial reform bill, quoted in *The New York Times* on April 23, 2010.

3. *www.politico.com/playbook/,* April 29, 2010.

4. These quotes from Representative Chris Van Hollen come from Mike Allen's *Playbook* for April 26, 2010. Along with an editorial in the Sunday *New York Times* of April 25, 2010, Mike Allen serves as a source for my description of the bill.

5. Below are some recent examples of this kind of investigative reporting:

   a. "Fact-Checking the US Chamber of Commerce: America's Most Overblown Business Lobby, Busted," by Josh Harkinson, *Mother Jones,* January/February 2010 Issue or see motherjones.com/authors/josh-harkinson.

   b. *Preaching Principle, Enabling Excess,* by Tom Donohue, released October 15, 2009; *Preaching Principle, Enabling Excess: How Tom Donohue Compromised the Credibility of the U.S. Chamber of Commerce* is a new report from Change to Win: *www.changetowin. org/chamber/?gclid=CPfB4euQmaECFR9aiAodgnjQPw*

   c. "Chamber of Commerce Admits Funding Anti-Worker Ads While Accepting Bailout Money," Adam Green, *The Huffington Post,* April 14, 2009.

6. Nicholas Thompson, "Era with No Name," *The New York Times Book Review*, August 3, 2008, p. 22.

7. *Newsweek*, Sept.1, 2008, p. 53.

8. Carla Marinucci, "Revamp Message, Experts Advise Slumping Obama," *The San Francisco Chronicle*, August 21, 2008, online archive.

CHAPTER 6: ON FRAMING PEACE

1. The latest testimony about this point comes from David Kilcullen and Andrew McDonald Exum in their May 17, 2009 *New York Times* Op-Ed, entitled "Death From Above, Outrage Down Below," on p. 13. I especially like their example of how we Americans would react if the police bombed the whole neighborhood in which a drug house was situated.

2. "Multimedia Taliban Get Their Message Across," by Nahal Toosi, *The San Francisco Chronicle*, May 17, 2009, online archive.

CHAPTER 8: ON FRAMING SOCIAL AND ECONOMIC JUSTICE

1. Four good sources for information about this kind of project are *YES! Magazine*, (*www.yesmagazine.org*), The Sustainable Communities Network, (*www.sustainable.org/*), New Village Press (*www. newvillagepress.net/index.php*), and New Village Journal (*www. newvillage.net/Journal/pastissues.html*)

2. Reports of cooperative resistance to foreclosures can be found at: *www.alternet.org/workplace/121844/resistance_to_ housing foreclosures_spreads_across_the_land/* and *www.nytimes.com/2009/02/18/nyregion/18foreclose.html*

3. Information about projects run by cities and counties is available at: *www.iclei.org/index.php?id=800.* In the San Francisco Bay Area, three major cities (San Jose, San Francisco, and Oakland) have just joined forces in a regional greening agenda: "Thinking Globally in the Bay Area," by Ron Dellums, Gavin Newsom and Chuck Reed, *San Francisco Chronicle*, March 6, 2009, online archive. Many American universities house institutes devoted to sustainable development at the regional level.

4. Other people who have already been working hard to prepare for those larger crises can provide us with good ideas and examples that we can easily adapt for the current wave. Some of those include the

Transition Towns phenomenon; it's worldwide, but here's the URL for the U.S. (*transitionus.ning.com*) and other groups like it, such as Community Solutions (*www.communitysolution.org/talks.html*). There are also recent books like *Small is Possible*, by Lyle Estill, about work in Chatham County, N.C., and *Plan C*, by Pat Murphy.

5. Thomas Homer-Dixon, "Our Panarchic Future," *World Watch*, March/April 2009, p. 15. *www.worldwatch.org/node/6008*

6. Ibid.

7. More information about Earth Overshoot can be found at the Global Footprint Network's page on this topic: *www.footprintnetwork.org/gfn_sub.php?content=overshoot*

PART III: HOW TO FRAME IT AMERICAN

1. Beginning in early spring 2010, reports of academic studies that critiqued brainstorming in business settings began to appear. Some of the most widely cited were "Teamwork, the True Mother of Invention," by Janet Rae-Dupree, *The New York Times*, December 07, 2008, and "Sometimes, It's Better to Brainstorm Alone," by Andrew O'Connell, on the *Research Blog* of the *Harvard Business Review*, February 4, 2010.

However, a close study of these results makes clear that the operative flaw was the problem of competitiveness in such venues, as individuals held back their own best ideas. Cooperative brainstorming in a nonprofit or activist setting is unlikely to feature individuals holding back their best ideas for personal gain. For this reason, current critiques of business group brainstorming do not apply to our Metaphor Project American Framing method.

An interesting new model of corporate brainstorming that does work very well was reported in *The New York Times Magazine* 2010 Year in Ideas issue, December 16, 2010. The article, "In Pursuit of the Perfect Brainstorm," by David Segal, described Jump Associates of San Mateo, California. Jump Associates is a consulting firm that does brainstorming work on behalf of corporations like Proctor & Gamble, Mars, and General Electric. This "outside team" model also protects the brainstorming process from damage by individuals refusing to share good ideas.

CHAPTER 9: AMERICAN FRAMING TOOLS THAT ADD OOMPH!

1. These Metaphor Project lists have been developed and validated through ongoing interdisciplinary research and experimentation. See the "American Studies" section in Resources for some of our sources.

CHAPTER 10: THE AMERICAN FRAMING STEPS: OUR SECRET

1. See Note 1 in the Introduction to Part III, on why the current critique of brainstorming applies only to highly competitive business settings.

2. See also Leslie Savan's study of "pop speak," *Slam Dunks and No-Brainers.*

3. Malcolm Gladwell, *Blink*, P. 11.

4. George Lakoff, *The Political Mind*, P. 9 and PP. 34–44.

5. See especially Patrick Reinsborough and Doyle Canning, *Re:Imagining Change.*

6. See Thom Hartmann's book, *Cracking the Code*, and his website: *www.thomhartmann.com*

APPENDIX I: FRAMES, FRAMING, AND METAPHOR TODAY

1. Anat Shenker–Osorio, in "Numbers and Sense," Netroots Nation 2011 Conference, *www.netrootsnation.org/node/1868*

2. My original theoretical approach in teaching framing was based on the 20th century "New Rhetoric" created by Kenneth Burke, Chaim Perelman, and I.A. Richards. Their work was the seedbed for the development of many contemporary theoretical approaches, including cognitive science. The work of Burke, Perelman and Richards is now also being carried forward by those who call themselves "cognitive rhetoricians." See the bibliography on this topic in the Resources section of this book, in the part called Framing and Cognitive Rhetoric.

CPSIA information can be obtained at www.ICGtesting.com
Printed in the USA
LVOW081700031012

301362LV00013B/77/P